Punishment in the Community:
The Future of Criminal Justice

Anne Worrall

LONGMAN
London and New York

Addison Wesley Longman Limited
Edinburgh Gate, Harlow
Essex CM20 2JE
United Kingdom
and Associated Companies throughout the world

Published in the United States of America
by Addison Wesley Longman, New York

First published 1997

ISBN 0 582-29305-7

British Library Cataloguing-in-Publication Data

A catalogue record for this book is available from the British Library

Library of Congress Cataloging-in-Publication Data

Worrall, Anne.
  Punishment in the community: the future of criminal justice/Anne Worrall.
    p. cm.
  Includes bibliographical references and index.
  ISBN 0-582-29305-7 (pbk)
  1. Community-based corrections--Great Britain.   2. Probation--Great Britain.
  I. Title.
HV9345.A5W67 1997
364.6'8--DC21   97-13487
                                                          CIP

Set by 7 in 10/11 Times
Produced through Longman Malaysia, PP

CONTENTS

ACKNOWLEDGEMENTS

Over the years many people have contributed indirectly to the ideas I have tried to develop in this book. I am particularly grateful to two Staffordshire senior probation officers – John Mood and Pauline Hill – for their friendship and encouragement throughout my career in the probation service and all the years since. Mike Worthington, now Chief Probation Officer of Northumbria, was a source of inspiration when we both worked on NAPO Training Committee and in Manchester. At Keele University, Mike Collison was a kindred spirit over many years. His tragic illness and premature death while I was writing this book set the project in its proper perspective. My academic managers, Paul Wilding, Chris Phillipson and Pat Carlen, have always had more faith in me than I deserve and I am privileged to have worked with them.

Finally, I am grateful to Jo Campling for her encouragement and advice on earlier drafts of the book.

INTRODUCTION

'Small earthquake in Peru – not many dead.'

It is not considered very exciting to talk about the extent to which criminals are *not* sent to prison. Rather like the apocryphal headline above, the subject is lacking in news value, unless one already has an association with it. Consequently, when compared with the vast literature on prisons, there has been very little written about non-custodial penal measures. There is no market for the autobiographies of offenders' experiences of community service. 'A woman on probation' would have sold rather less well than 'A woman in custody' (Peckham 1985).

Contemporary political (and academic) debate tends to assume that penality is synonymous with prison and that the most important theoretical and policy questions revolve around the nature, number and treatment of the (predominantly male) criminals sent to prison by our courts. Much attention has also been paid to the symbolism of the prison and its disciplinary effect on the populace at large. Penal measures which do not involve incarceration tend to be regarded by most criminologists as monolithic, unproblematic and invariably preferable to prison. Students consider them to be of only marginal and specialist interest.

Within the probation service there has always been much introspective analysis of the balance that can and should be maintained between caring for the offenders and controlling them. A perennial essay question set for trainee probation officers asks 'Is the probation service still a social work agency?', the implication being that its 'value base' is no longer compatible with the ethics of social work and that it is moving inexorably towards the American model of a corrections agency.

But that debate has been largely conducted within an apolitical framework that takes criminal justice policy as 'given' and which sees the role of the service as that of adapting to, or at least surviving, the vagaries of that ever-changing policy. Such debate is epitomised by the picture on the cover of one practice guide (Raynor, Smith and Vanstone 1994), which shows a probation officer and an offender standing outside a prison gate. The image is powerful yet contradictory. The offender is outside the prison, the prison is behind the offender, but the image of the prison is integral to the message that is to be conveyed. Probation is always practised in the shadow of prison.

About one and a half million people are sentenced for criminal offences every year in magistrates' courts and crown courts in England

and Wales (Home Office 1995a). A further 300,000 who admit their guilt and are considered suitable for police cautioning never reach court. Of all these people, fewer than 70,000 were sent to prison in 1994. Of the others, 130,000 received supervised community sentences and the vast majority of the rest were either fined (1 million) or discharged (130,000), which means that they were reprimanded and warned of harsher consequences for any future criminal activity.

It is certainly not the purpose of this book to argue that concern about the increasing number of offenders being sent to prison is misplaced. On the contrary, its central argument is that we are so obsessed with the belief that imprisonment is the only 'real' punishment for 'crime' (and we rarely bother to define these terms with any care) that we are incapable of conceptualising other penalties except in terms of their relationship to prison. We talk of 'non-custodial' sentences and 'alternatives to prison' and imply that anything less than total loss of liberty must be merely 'a soft option'. Yet, as even the crudest of official statistics demonstrate, the vast majority of people who break the law – and get caught – still never go anywhere near the gates of a prison. And we would be outraged if it were suggested that they should!

It follows that any analysis of the role of non-incarcerative sanctions must go beyond technical discussions of their effectiveness (for instance, in reducing reoffending) by comparison with imprisonment and must address their social meaning. What, to use Garland's phrase (1990) are the 'moral values and sensibilities' which such sanctions encapsulate (or fail to encapsulate)? What are their sources of authority and from whence do they gain their (lack of) social support? In short, it must explore the conundrum posed by the widespread usage of penal measures which are discursively impotent. It needs to ponder Windlesham's observation that:

if the belief, which had obtained such a hold on the British mind, that imprisonment was the only real punishment for criminal offences and anything else was a soft option was to be loosened, arguments with the power of dynamite were called for.   (Windlesham 1993:253)

Society's ambivalence towards punishment that does not involve prison can only be understood in the context of its deep-seated and increasing cynicism of the language of rationalisation. Non-incarcerative sanctions involve all the symbols of the modern state which arouse most suspicion – bureaucracy, professional power, unchallengable claims to expertise, lack of public accountability – in an area of human experience which arouses extreme (if irrational) emotions of fear and anger. Far from being viewed as 'an index of the refinement and civility attained by criminal justice', such measures are deemed to have redefined the social meaning of punishment in such a way that it has 'been removed from direct public participation and involvement and . . . cast in a form which de-emphasises [its] moral content' (Garland 1990:184–5).

We have no generic term for such punishment that does not involve reference to prison. Each measure has its own name but, as we shall see in Chapter 1, the absence of a collective noun which is not ineluctably hitched up to incarceration means that our analysis is conceptually impoverished. We simply cannot think about punishment without thinking about prison because we do not have the words with which to do it.

The phrase 'Punishment in the Community' entered penal vocabulary with the government's Green Paper, *Punishment, Custody and the Community* (Home Office 1988). It was a deliberate attempt to dislodge prison from its central position in penal thinking. The reasons for this conceptual shift under a Conservative government (and the subsequent backlash) are complex and will be discussed later in Chapters 2 and 3 but the phrase has come to signify a specific period of criminal justice policy-making in the late 1980s, culminating in the Criminal Justice Act 1991. According to Windlesham's account (1993), the architect of these developments was the then Home Secretary, Douglas Hurd, assisted by the then Minister of State, John Patten.

By the time the Criminal Justice Act 1991 was drafted, the phrase 'community sentences' had emerged but this referred only to sentences involving supervision by the probation service – probation and supervision orders, community service orders and the new combination orders. In the new sentencing framework, fines and discharges were each categorised separately.

Other attempts to find a generic term have included 'community corrections' (Haxby 1978), 'community based penalties' (National Association for the Care and Resettlement of Offenders (NACRO) 1989) and 'community punishments' (von Hirsch and Ashworth 1992). All have apparently considered the use of the word 'community' to be unproblematic. But 'community' has become a thoroughly promiscuous word, attaching itself to almost any activity formerly regarded as a responsibility of the state – and for a very cheap price. The significance of its usage in criminal justice discourse will be explored in Chapter 4.

Creeping into penal vocabulary from American literature are the terms 'intermediate sanctions' (see, for example, Tonry and Hamilton 1995) and, more chillingly, 'smart sentencing' (Byrne, Lurigio and Petersilia 1992). The latter phrase has been described as being 'the penal version of the neutron bomb which leaves the offender intact but destroys the offending behaviour' (Oldfield 1993:32). Such terms refer to sentencing options which are intended to hold the middle ground between incarceration and what might be termed 'regular' probation, the latter being regarded as a welfare-orientated rather than punitive measure. They are characterised by intensive supervision, surveillance and carefully targeted rehabilitative programmes, such as those to be discussed in Chapter 8. Such sanctions have as their stated aims (see Byrne, Lurigio and Petersilia 1992:ix–x):

- to save taxpayers money by providing cost-effective alternatives to prison;
- to deter offenders and others from crime;

- to protect the community by exercising more control than does traditional supervision; and
- to rehabilitate offenders by using mandatory requirements and by the swift revocation of violated orders.

The unstated but equally important aims, according to Byrne *et al.* are:

- to create an 'appearance' of correctional reform;
- to find a way of reclaiming limited resources for non-custodial sentences; and
- to enable probation administrators and politicians to respond to the punitive mood of the public.

The aim of this book, therefore, is to unravel the complex of institutional goals (the role of community punishment in the criminal justice system), professional goals (what can be achieved by community punishment) and political goals (the packaging and 'sale' of community punishment to the 'law-abiding' public). Central to this analysis is the changing role of the probation service and its relationship to the courts, which will be examined in Chapters 5, 6 and 7. By way of illustrating these changes, Chapters 9 and 10 will discuss changing attitudes to two particular groups of offenders: sex offenders and juveniles. The concluding chapter will consider the futures of community punishment in the twenty-first century.

The phrase 'Punishment in the Community' will be used to refer to the political and academic discourses which underpin discussions of non-incarcerative punishment, and the phrase 'community punishments' to refer to the concrete penal measures. The phrases are not mutually exclusive, as it is impossible to examine any discourse without also examining its effects in practice, but the distinction may be a useful one in making accessible the various elements of this complicated and under-theorised area of penality. The constraints of existing vocabulary will be identified and interrogated as the book progresses.

The first such constraint is that of gender. Throughout this book, the masculine pronoun will predominate and this is quite deliberate. Men who are cautioned or sentenced for criminal offences outnumber women by at least four to one and the difference increases with the severity of the offence. For example, one in ten violent offenders and one in forty burglars are women (as also are one in nine motoring offenders!). Sentencing patterns indicate that, while one in five offenders fined or placed on probation are women, only one in fifteen community service orders or combination orders are made on women (Home Office 1994a). Crime remains overwhelmingly a male activity and community punishment, like prison, is a response to male offending. This does not mean that this book will ignore women. On the contrary, it aims to examine the gendered nature of community punishment and to argue that a fully social analysis of community punishment must take account of community attitudes not only towards men and women who offend, but also towards the kinds of punishment which we, as men and women, wish to endorse as contributing to the wellbeing of the community.

PART ONE

THE PRINCIPLES AND POLITICS OF COMMUNITY PUNISHMENT

CHAPTER 1

Introducing community punishment

Introduction

In attempting to provide a framework for understanding punishments that do not involve prison, in their own right, there is a danger of imposing a false coherence and rationale on a set of experiences and events which have neither. But not to do so simply perpetuates the lack of interest and analysis which currently characterise the field. It is not without significance that Cohen's *Visions of Social Control* (1985), which warns of a dispersal of discipline from inside the prison out into the community remains a more seductive text than Bottoms' more staid analysis of 'Neglected features of contemporary penal systems' (1983). The latter suggests that at least some of our most widely used punishments have very little to do with the creation of docile, compliant bodies and much more to do with penalising rule infringement, much as one might in a game of ice hockey (Bottoms 1983:176). It will not do, he argues, to make sweeping generalisations about non-incarcerative sanctions, whether those be of the 'soft option' or the 'punitive city' variety. But neither will it do, in reacting against such generalisation, to succumb to a nihilistic parody of postmodern analysis which claims that there are no identifiable themes, no patterns or consistencies – only gaps, illogicalities and fragmentations.

To make a start, then, it is possible to categorise community punishments in such a way as to enable an analysis of some underlying assumptions about the relationship between the state and the individual.

From segregation to normalisation: the birth of community punishment

Before the end of the nineteenth century, the only non-custodial sentences (apart from the death penalty) used regularly by the courts were fines and release on recognisances (such as binding over, whose origins lie in the Justice of the Peace Act 1361). Since there were no facilities for paying fines by instalments, however, many people were imprisoned for non-payment of fines (Garland 1985). Release on recognisance usually involved giving sureties to guarantee future behaviour (rather like the present-day conditional discharge) or being 'vouched for' by a respectable citizen. Such undertakings were often given by the Police

Court Missionaries, founded in 1876 by the Church of England Temperance Society and seen as the forerunners of the modern probation officer. The primary issues in imposing punishment, however, were concerns for formal equality before the law, uniformity of treatment and proportionality in the severity of punishment (Garland 1985).

During the period 1895–1914, however, there was a transformation in the relationship between criminals and the state. An increasing confidence in both their material wealth and their scientific knowledge led the late Victorians and the Edwardians to believe that crime was a social disease for which a cure was possible through 'specific practices of normalization, classification, categorization and discrimination between criminal types' (Garland 1985:32). The reasons for such a transformation lie deep in the changing nature of Victorian industrial society and, in particular, attitudes towards the poor, but the result was the development of a complete sphere of punishment which focused on social control through attention to the material, social and psychological welfare of criminals.

By the second decade of the twentieth century, there was a separate court to deal with juveniles (The Children Act 1908), a separate training institution (Borstal) for juveniles (The Prevention of Crime Act 1908), a professional service to supervise offenders in the community (The Probation of Offenders Act 1907) and a means for paying fines by instalments (The Criminal Justice Administration Act 1914). Special institutional provision was also made for inebriates (The Inebriates Act 1898) and for mentally defective criminals (The Mental Deficiency Act 1913).

Since that time, the most significant developments in community sentencing before the Criminal Justice Act 1991 have been the introduction of conditional discharges, attendance centres (Criminal Justice Act 1948, which also abolished birching), police cautioning (Children and Young Person Act 1969) and community service (Criminal Justice Act 1972). Compensation orders became sentences in their own right in 1988.

It is possible, therefore, to identify themes around which to organise community punishment conceptually. Those themes are:

- Self-regulatory penalties;
- Financial penalties;
- Supervisory penalties.

Self-regulatory penalties

The thread which joins police cautions and court discharges is the assumption that identification as a wrong-doer is sufficient to prevent further misbehaviour. Denunciation (which is private in the case of cautions but public in the case of discharges) of an otherwise upright citizen who has breached his contract with the local community (and thus with society) is seen to be enough to shame and reintegrate him with that community (Braithwaite 1989). He admits his guilt – or is found guilty – and he frequently apologises and promises never to do it again. His word is accepted (though often on condition that he proves his sincerity by not reoffending within a fixed period of time).

Financial penalties

The relationship between money and punishment, though ill-defined, is long established (see, for example, the Book of Exodus in the Old Testament) and taken for granted. The fine remains the most popular sentence imposed by courts, although its proportionate use has declined (Newburn 1995). It is regarded by many as the most flexible of sentences since courts can match its amount both to the seriousness of the offence and to the offender's ability to pay (though in practice these two principles are often in conflict). At the same time, it is an impersonal sanction, implying no personal stigma. It is the only punishment whose obligations can be met by someone other than the offender himself. It does not matter who pays the fine, as long as it is paid. So, while financial punishment may be effective in preventing further offending because 'it hits them where it hurts – in the pocket', it is not always seen as holding the offender sufficiently accountable for his breach of contract with the community. For this reason, it lacks the moral censure and personalised infliction of pain perceived to be essential in the punishment of serious crime (Young 1989).

This concern may be met to some extent through the payment of compensation, which may be linked to other sentences or (since 1988) imposed as a sentence in its own right. Compensation requires the offender to confront the harm done to his victim in a more direct way than a fine does, but the problem of devising a formula for the relationship between money and harm done (except in the most straightforward cases of theft or damage) is even more acute.

Supervisory penalties

The assumption underlying all punishments which involve an element of supervision is that the offender lacks the motivation or personal resources to repair his breach of contract with the community unaided. The exact nature of that aid is highly contested and its examination forms the central concern of this book. At this stage, therefore, it is perhaps sufficient to identify the main supervisory punishments as:

- the probation order (which may include additional conditions relating to medical treatment, accommodation or activities and is available for anyone over 16 years of age);
- the supervision order (a similar order available for anyone under 18 years of age);

- the curfew order (restricting physical liberty with or without the addition of electronic monitoring or 'tagging');
- the attendance centre order (requiring fortnightly attendance for sessions of two or three hours, involving physical and educational activity run by the police and used mostly for young people);
- the community service order (undertaking unpaid work for up to 240 hours and available for anyone over 16 years of age); and
- the combination order (which combines elements of probation and community service).

Other sentences

There are other punishments which do not fall neatly into any of these categories. Binding over, for example, is self-regulatory in that it accepts a verbal undertaking from the offender, but it requires a financial forfeit if that undertaking is broken. A deferred sentence (introduced under the Powers of the Criminal Courts Act 1973) offers a period of self-regulation to the offender – time to 'put his house in order' – but requires a return to court after that time with no guarantee of the nature of the eventual punishment. The suspended prison sentence might be regarded by some as self-regulatory in so far as no immediate pain, other than shaming, is inflicted on the offender. Nevertheless, the threat of imprisonment in the future is made more explicitly than in any other punishment, and the offender is left in no doubt that he has narrowly escaped incarceration, thus rendering the notion of self-regulation rather secondary to that of involuntary self-restriction. The use of the suspended prison sentence has declined and now represents only 1 per cent of all sentences (Newburn 1995).

A hospital order relates specifically to offenders diagnosed as being mentally disordered and may be regarded, in theory, as being 'somewhere between' supervision and prison. In practice, however, many of these 'patients' experience imprisonment at some stage of the criminal justice process, either pre-trial or following sentence. The numbers of those who do not and are sentenced to 'unrestricted' hospital orders have remained steady at about 750 per year since 1984. Numbers receiving 'restricted' hospital orders (which frequently, though not necessarily, involve prison, secure units or special hospitals) have increased over the past ten years with annual admissions quadrupling from 284 in 1984 to 1108 in 1994 (Home Office 1995b).

Principles of sentencing and community punishment

Having identified the range of community disposals available to the courts, the next stage is to see the extent to which they can be said to satisfy the requirements of conventional 'philosophies of punishment' and 'principles of sentencing'.

It is usually argued that there are two broad philosophies of punishment known as **retributivism** and **utilitarianism**. Put very simply, retributivism (which can be traced back to ancient legal systems) maintains that punishing wrong-doing is a moral right and duty, an end in itself and an essential component of a civilised society. The obligations on the punisher are to ensure, first, that the person to be punished is correctly identified (that is, that guilt is established) and, second, that the punishment is proportionate to the seriousness of the crime (that is, that it is not excessive). Utilitarianism (whose most eloquent exponent was the philosopher Jeremy Bentham 1748–1832) maintains that punishment is itself an evil which can only be justified if it brings about a greater good, namely the reduction of crime. Punishment is a means to an end, not an end in itself. The most obvious distinction between the two philosophies is that utilitarians have to demonstrate that punishment (or sentences) work, while retributivists only have to demonstrate that punishment is deserved.

There has been a tendency to associate retributivism with measures that are predominantly punitive, such as imprisonment and corporal punishment, and to associate utilitarianism with rehabilitative measures, but this oversimplifies the relationships. From these two broad philosophical approaches, a number of principles have developed which often result in contradictory and inconsistent sentencing. The implications for community punishment of the received wisdom of sentencing 'principles' require some examination.

Just deserts   implies that the main purpose of sentencing is to denounce the crime and 'visit retribution' on the criminal, to the extent that he deserves it. (Retribution must be distinguished from revenge, which is disproportionate punishment and supposedly has no place in any modern philosophy of justice, though observers of the tabloid press may wonder otherwise.) The crucial considerations are the seriousness of the crime and the culpability of the criminal (that is, the extent to which he can be held responsible for his actions). There is scope to consider aggravating and mitigating factors in so far as they relate to the offence and the offender's part in it, but wider considerations of the offender's circumstances are deemed to be less relevant. The government White Paper *Crime, Justice and Protecting the Public* (Home Office, 1990a) sets out the philosophy underpinning the Criminal Justice Act 1991 and states that its aim

is to ensure that convicted criminals ... are punished justly and suitably according to the seriousness of their offences; in other words that they should get their just deserts.   (para. 2.1)

It goes on to explain that this means that, while serious offenders should still go to prison, many others can be dealt with safely (and more cheaply) in the community

Deterrence was the original concern underlying utilitarianism. It implies that the main purpose of sentencing is to deter people from committing crime. There are two elements in this principle: individual and general deterrence. Individual deterrence refers to measures which are intended to impress on the offender that the personal consequences of his actions in the form of the punishment received make it 'not worth' committing crime again. The most commonly used individually deterrent sentence is the fine, but any sentence which restricts offenders' liberty, inconveniences or shames them may have a deterrent effect. General deterrence refers to measures which are intended to set an example for other people in the hope of deterring them from committing crime. For example, a bout of criminal damage in a particular locality may result in an 'exemplary' prison sentence to demonstrate that local people have 'had enough'. One objection to deterrent sentences is that they may be disproportionate to the seriousness of the offence, in order to 'make a point'. A more fundamental criticism is the underlying assumption that crime is committed as a rational choice, with the offender weighing up the possible consequences of his actions before deciding to offend. Although this may be true in some instances, it is by no means the only explanation for offending. Much crime is impulsive or stems from what most people would view as irrational thoughts or feelings.

Protection and incapacitation are aims intended to protect the public from further harm from the offender. Rather than relying on the rational judgement of the offender that 'crime does not pay', a safer way of ensuring that no further crime is committed is to reduce the opportunity for crime by restricting the offender's liberty. The ultimate example of such a sentence is the death penalty. Imprisonment is less effective, since prisoners may escape and they will, in any case, be released at some point. Giving someone a community service order, sending them to a probation centre or even subjecting them to electronic monitoring may seem mild measures in comparison but the principles of restriction and surveillance are basically the same. The extent of the restriction has to be decided according to the seriousness of the offence and this means that the retributive principle of proportionality also has to play a part.

Compensation and reparation Just as deterrence may be either individual or general, so the principle of 'making good' harm done can include both the individual victim and wider society. Compensation (predominantly financial) is usually made to the individual victim of a crime. Reparation is a broader concept which involves the offender in doing something socially useful and morally exculpatory (such as community service), thereby demonstrating his remorse and willingness to put back something into society.

Reform, rehabilitation and correction Bringing about fundamental changes to the personality, attitudes and behaviour of offenders, so that they no longer commit offences, not because they fear the possible consequences but because they appreciate that crime is wrong, has long been a utilitarian aim of sentencing. The distinction between reform and rehabilitation is not an easy one. Reform tends to assume that the individual has free will and is therefore capable of changing his attitudes and beliefs, given the right stimulus. As Hudson puts it: 'The criminal can repent, can become a good citizen, if only he will'(1987:3). Rehabilitation assumes that the individual is determined more by circumstances (personal, social or medical) and that a change in these is required in order to produce a change in behaviour. 'Correction' is a term that has been imported from America. For some people, it has unacceptable overtones of coercion but Walker (1991) argues that it is a 'non-committal word' which we are adopting wisely because it implies an appropriate humility about the state of our knowledge about the reasons for which people stop committing crimes. In the past, people have viewed crime variously as a symptom of sin (which only religious conversion will remedy) or disease (which only medical science will cure) or an emotionally deprived childhood (which only psycho-therapeutic casework will resolve) or poverty (which only social and political action will alleviate). While all these explanations might provide some insight into understanding some crime, none provides a full explanation and few people now believe that such an explanation is either possible or desirable. People commit crimes for many reasons. They also stop committing crimes for many reasons and the sentence they receive may be only one (and possibly the least significant) of several influential factors.

Obstacles to community punishment

✳ Attempts to uncouple the discourses of community punishment and imprisonment run into a number of recurring obstacles. First, and most familiar, is the obstacle of public and media perceptions that the demands of punishment can only be properly met, at the very least, by imprisonment (and for some only by the return of the death penalty). The principles on which state punishment is traditionally founded are interpreted within popular discourse as referring to corporal and incarcerative punishment. Other measures are viewed as poor substitutes, suitable only for the very young, the very old and the feeble-minded (and not even always for those categories, as will be seen in Chapters 9 and 10). Entangled with this popular reluctance to legitimise community punishment is the legacy of the Victorian principle of 'less eligibility'. Underlying all nineteenth century institutional provision for the 'undeserving' was the belief that the standard of life enjoyed by inmates should not be greater than that of the poorest 'respectable' citizen. 'Less eligibility' remains a tenacious precept in penal thinking and surfaces in community punishment when offenders are perceived to be given better opportunities (for work, education or recreation) than the poorest non-offender.

Second is the obstacle of unfair or inconsistent sentencing. Despite increasingly sophisticated guidelines about the use of community sentences, there remain concerns that certain groups of offenders are over-represented in prison for reasons that have little to do with the nature of their offences. Community sentences, it is argued, are reserved in practice for those who are relatively advantaged socially – for those who have sufficient money to pay a fine, for those who are employed, for those who are perceived by probation officers to be able to 'benefit' from supervision, and so on. In other words, community sentences run the risk of being discriminatory, of being seen as justice for white middle-class criminals.

Third is the obstacle of 'net-widening', a term which entered criminal justice vocabulary in the 1960s in the wake of labelling theory. With the proliferation of alternatives to custody, so the argument goes, comes the danger that instead of keeping more people out of prison, community sentences will simply draw more and more people into the 'net' of the criminal justice system and thereby increase the likelihood that they will eventually end up in prison. The treatment of juvenile offenders in the 1970s illustrates the point. Following the introduction of police cautioning with the Children and Young Person Act 1969, the numbers of juveniles being cautioned rose steadily but so too did the numbers being placed under supervision and the numbers being sent to detention centres and borstals. Without the political will to reduce the number of offenders sent into custody, the introduction of more intermediate sanctions tends to raise rather than lower the punitive stakes.

Fourth, and finally, is the obstacle of enforcement. Fines are all very well if they are paid. Probation is all very well if appointments are kept. Community service is all very well if the work is done. But what if it is not? Surely, it is argued, community sentences must ultimately be 'backed up' with prison? There has to be a sentence of last resort for those who abuse the alternative opportunities they are given.

Probation officers are notoriously reluctant to institute 'breach proceedings' against offenders who fail to comply with the requirements of probation orders and fewer than 3 per cent of probation orders are terminated for this reason annually (Home Office 1994b). Many officers see 'failure to comply' (which usually means failing to keep appointments) as a reflection on either their own inability to establish a helping relationship with the offender or on the offender's chaotic lifestyle (Kirwin 1985). Returning an offender to court, with the possibility of a consequent prison sentence, is not an action which most officers relish, though some see it as an effective exercise of their authority, especially if they can persuade the court to allow the probation order to continue (Lawson 1978; Drakeford 1993). Breach enthusiasm is slightly more evident in relation to community service orders, where approximately 16 per cent of orders each year are terminated for 'failure to comply' (Home Office 1994b). 'Failure to comply' in this context usually means non-attendance at work and this is arguably a more measurable and less personalised omission than is failure to engage in a therapeutic relationship)

The enforcement of fines is an even less personalised process, though that seems to be no guarantee of its equity. Imprisonment for fine default is an extraordinarily expensive form of enforcement and courts would argue that they avoid it wherever possible, preferring to make money payment supervision orders (using probation officers to give advice and encourage payment) or attachment of earnings orders (stopping money out of pay packets). Nevertheless, about 20 per cent of prison receptions are fine defaulters and although most only spend a few days in prison (and therefore account for less than 2 per cent of the prison population overall), most studies show that the vast majority of these are unable, rather than unwilling, to pay their fines (Cavadino and Dignan 1992).

Discrimination, criminal justice and community punishment

As we have seen, the main criticism of utilitarianism is that it takes insufficient account of the relationship between punishment and the seriousness of the crime. The main criticism of retributivism is that it takes insufficient account of the effect of punishment. Both approaches run the risk, for different reasons, of making sentencing distinctions which are based on what are termed 'improper grounds'. By either taking account of, or failing to take account of, the range of personal and social factors which surround the commission of crime, sentencers and those who advise them are frequently accused of being unfair, inconsistent and discriminatory.

Since the mid-1980s, particular concerns have emerged about the over-representation of black people in prison and the inappropriate treatment of female offenders. In both cases, it is argued that sentencers and professional workers display discriminatory attitudes, based on stereotypical views of black people and women who commit crimes.

Concern about discrimination in the criminal justice system led the government to include a section (s.95) in the Criminal Justice Act 1991 which requires the Home Secretary to publish information annually which will enable those administering the system to avoid discrimination 'on the ground of sex or race or any other improper ground'. Critics point out that the drafting of the section makes this optional, since the Home Secretary has the incongruous alternative option of publishing information to assist administrators 'to become aware of the financial implications of their decisions'.

Discrimination on grounds of race

Black people (by which term is meant non-white minority ethnic groups of Afro-Caribbean and Asian origin) appear to be involved disproportionately in the criminal justice system as both offenders and victims of crime, though not as workers. Relative to their numbers in the population of England and Wales (5–6 per cent), black people (and especially those of Afro-Caribbean origin) are over-represented in prison. In 1995, 17 per cent of the male and 24 per cent of the female prison population were non-white (though it is important to note that 30 per cent of these males and 52 per cent of these females are foreign nationals, according to Home Office Statistical Bulletin 14/96). The over-representation of black people in prison raises two questions: do black people commit more crime than white people and/or are black people discriminated against by the criminal justice system? (Cavadino and Dignan 1992; Harris 1992).

Those who argue that black people commit disproportionate amounts of crime range from those who claim that black people are biologically more inclined than white people to commit crime through those who argue that black people born in England and Wales tend to grow up without respect for 'British' ways, authority or law, to those who argue that the experiences of direct and indirect discrimination (that is, less employment, poorer housing and more poverty) make it more likely that black people will engage in criminal activity. It is not difficult to identify such beliefs as being racist, because they are based on prejudiced assumptions about a whole group of people which could never be shown to be true by objective enquiry. Pearson (1983) demonstrates that generations of white people have always maintained that Britain is 'by nature' a peaceful and law-abiding place and that they have always chosen to blame crime and public disorder on 'foreigners' (particularly young men) with 'alien cultures'.

There is more evidence, however, that black people tend to attract more attention and suspicion than white people, particularly from the police and particularly in public places. A number of research studies (predominantly in London) have indicated that black people (particularly those of Afro-Caribbean origin) are more likely than white people to be stopped and searched by the police and more likely to be arrested (Reiner 1989). There is also some evidence that black young people are less likely than their white counterparts to receive a caution and no further action. (One reason for this might be that the young black person denies committing the offence and therefore considers their arrest unjustified; the police, however, may then feel obliged to proceed with the charge.) Research suggests that interaction between police officers and black people is influenced by a 'canteen culture' based on racist banter and prejudiced stereotyping of black people (Lea and Young 1984).

Black defendants are more likely than whites to be committed to crown court for trial but this is often by their own choice because they deny the offence and believe they will get fairer treatment from a jury trial. Unfortunately, however, if they are found guilty, they are likely to receive a harsher sentence than they would in a magistrates' court. It has been difficult to find clear evidence that race plays an influential part in sentencing in the crown court but a study by Hood (1992) appears to demonstrate that at least some of the difference between the numbers of black men in the population at large and the numbers in prison can be accounted for by differential sentencing of black and white defendants. Hood claimed to find no similar evidence in relation to black women, a large proportion of whom he found to be drug couriers and therefore likely to be dealt with harshly for that reason alone.

Hood also confirmed previous findings that black men were less likely than white men to be given community punishments such as probation orders or community service orders. This appears to be partly due to a inability on the part of probation officers to make convincing recommendations for such options (Denney 1992).

Discrimination is usually seen to be cumulative rather than specific at any one stage of the process but probation officers may be making a significant contribution. Unlike studies on women offenders, however, the level of analysis has been rather simplistic – either black people are actually committing more crime than white people, as a result of their experiences of racism, or racism is responsible for constructing black people as being more criminal than white people (or, occasionally, as in Lea and Young 1984, the two arguments are combined to suggest a vicious circle). The focus has been on social reaction rather than an exploration of etiology. Two notable exceptions have been the work of John Pitts (1986,1993) who has consistently rooted discussion of racism in understandings about youth justice and social inequality, and David Denney (1992) who has utilised discourse analysis to deconstruct professional assessments of black offenders and to provide insight into the difficulties which (white) probation officers have in transforming the black offender into the

'good subject' who can be conceptualised as having the 'potential' to become structured into and identify with probation discourses.   (Denney 1992:128)

Discrimination on grounds of sex

We do not know why there is apparently such a great difference between men and women in relation to criminal behaviour. Some people believe that men are genetically more aggressive and inclined towards deviant behaviour. Others argue that the difference is caused by differences of socialisation. Girls tend to be brought up to be more conforming and to behave in ways that will not get them into trouble with the law. It is often assumed that adolescent girls are more likely to be 'in moral danger' because of sexual promiscuity than to become involved in criminal activity. When they are adults, women may have less opportunity to commit crimes because they are looking after their homes and their children. If they cannot cope with these responsibilities, they are more likely to seek medical or psychiatric help than to turn to crime. Heidensohn (1985) describes the ways in which modern society controls women's behaviour by communicating expectations that women will be feminine and domesticated. Some writers (see Adler 1975) thought that women's liberation would mean more women committing more serious violent crime but, despite media encouragement of a moral panic, this has not happened (see Chapter 10). Although more women are committing crime, in absolute numbers, it is generally less serious than that committed by men. The biggest increase in women's crime over the past ten years has been not having a television licence!

Because so few women commit crime, it has been argued that women criminals are also abnormal women. Some people think there must be something biologically or mentally wrong with women who commit crime. In particular, they think that women criminals are 'more masculine' than 'normal' women. Others believe that women commit crime because they suffer from premenstrual tension, the menopause or postnatal depression. Yet others argue that women commit crime because they are sexually promiscuous or emotionally unbalanced. Although all these explanations may apply in a few individual cases, there is no evidence to support these ideas as general theories of female offending. (All these theories are discussed in detail in many texts on women and crime – for example, Heidensohn 1985; Morris 1987.)

Carlen (1988) is one of several contemporary writers who argue that many of the women who commit crimes do so because they are poor. They steal food and clothes, often for their children, and defraud Social Security because they cannot live on the money they get. A lot of women in prison have been in care as children and find that they cannot look after themselves, as adults, on their own. Often they are homeless and sometimes they have drug or alcohol problems. Some women commit crimes out of greed or for excitement, just like some men, but these are a very small number. Women who commit violent crimes often do so after years of physical or emotional abuse. Of recent years, a number of foreign women have been imprisoned for acting as drugs couriers, often under duress or as a result of poverty.

At first sight it may appear that female offenders are treated more leniently by the police and the courts than male offenders. In 1990, just under half were cautioned by the police (and not brought to court) compared with a third of male offenders. Of those brought to court, 34 per cent of women were given discharges (compared with 15 per cent of men) and 19 per cent were put on supervision or probation (compared with 10 per cent of men). On the other hand, 41 per cent of men were fined (compared with 31 per cent of women) and 8 per cent of men were given community service orders (compared with 4 per cent of women). Finally, 17 per cent of men and 6 per cent of women were sent to prison. One compilation of official statistics by Hedderman and Hough (1994) at the Home Office Research Unit argues that there is no evidence to support the claim that women are systematically dealt with more severely than men and that, overall, women seem more likely to receive lenient sentences even when previous convictions are taken into consideration. They do, however, concede that this does not rule out the possibility of disparities within gender and that individual women may receive unusually harsh treatment.

Indeed, there may be a number of reasons for this apparent leniency. If a woman gets a 'light' sentence it is usually because her offence is not very serious. Occasionally a woman gets off 'lightly' because a magistrate thinks she is a good wife and mother – a respectable woman who has made one mistake. Magistrates often think that they are being kind to women by putting them on probation because they think it will help them to have someone to talk to. And often it does. Unfortunately, however, being on probation may have a stigmatising and 'net-widening' effect on a woman, making it more likely that she will go to prison if she commits another offence. Men often get the chance to do community service or go to special day activities in a probation centre, which tend to be considered unsuitable for women. Women also get sent to hospital for psychiatric reports more often than men. Allen (1987) argues that psychiatrists seem very ready to label female offenders as 'mentally ill'.

There is evidence, however, that some women get heavier sentences than they should because magistrates think that women should not commit crime – that they are setting a bad example to their children and not behaving like proper women. Unmarried or divorced women, women with children in care and black women appear to get heavier sentences. They seem to get punished for who they are, rather than for what they have done. As we have seen, one quarter of women in prison are black, which is far in excess of their proportion in the population outside prison. Some of these women are drugs couriers who will be deported when they finish their sentence and may have to serve another sentence in their own country. But many black women in prison were born in Great Britain and commit the same offences as white women.

When the Criminal Justice Act 1991 was first implemented, there was some optimism that 'just deserts' for women would actually result in less punishment (because women commit less serious offences and have fewer previous convictions than men) and better provision (because access to community punishments had to be non-discriminatory according to section 95 of the Act). But the amendments of 1993 (see Chapter 3) and a wilful misinterpretation of 'equal opportunities' rhetoric has led to a rapid expansion of the female prison population and a reduction in the numbers of women receiving community punishments, especially the traditional probation order.

Discrimination on grounds of class

While attention has been focused rightly on discrimination against black people and women in recent years, it could be argued that class discrimination in the criminal justice system is so overwhelming as to be taken for granted. The vast majority of defendants appearing in court are from the working or unemployed classes, to the extent that some writers (such as Murray 1990) argue that there now exists an 'underclass' of poor, homeless and/or unemployed people with unstable family relationships who are responsible for most of the crime and disorder in our society. The first *National Prison Survey* (Walmsley, Howard and White 1992) indicated that people with these characteristics in their backgrounds are over-represented in prison. Critics of underclass theory point out that people in every social class commit crime and that the crime which damages society most is often committed by very rich people. The fact that lower-class crime is the most stigmatised is itself a form of discrimination. Gardiner argues that the Criminal Justice Act 1991 and its advocacy of punishment in the community was in reality 'a response in terms of the management of an aggregate group of people rather than individuals' (1995:363). It is, he argues, the 'underclass' which is being targeted by contemporary penal policy.

Conclusion

This chapter has introduced the reader to the range of community punishments, their origins, development and use. It has included a discussion of the relationship between traditional sentencing principles and contemporary political debates about community punishment. But the analysis has also demonstrated some of the recurrent problems associated with non-incarcerative disposals, such as net-widening, enforcement, the image of the 'soft option' and the potential for discrimination on grounds of race, gender and class.

CHAPTER 2

From alternatives to custody to punishment in the community

We should eschew the phrase 'alternatives to custody' for that acts subliminally to suggest that custody is the real answer and produces an expectation that we will supply a kind of custody in the community.   (Lacey 1984:105)

Introduction

The early 1980s saw a number of apparently disparate political and academic developments which nevertheless worked together to suggest a strengthening of community punishment and an optimism about reducing the prison population and improving prison conditions. Attacks on the rehabilitative potential of institutions from across the political spectrum, centralising tendencies on the part of the Home Office and concern within the probation service to resist marginalisation, together resulted in the discourse of 'alternatives to custody' in the mid-1980s and eventually to the idea of Punishment in the Community and the Criminal Justice Act 1991.

The demise of the rehabilitative ideal

Until the late 1960s, rehabilitation had been the dominant principle of criminal justice. It was an optimistic approach which held that offenders committed crimes for reasons rooted in their biological and psychological make-up or their social upbringing and that, with sufficient knowledge and patience, they could be cured of their criminal tendencies.

But that ideal came increasingly under attack from a number of directions. Loss of confidence in the treatment approach to deviance control, coupled with the rising influence of interactionist and Marxist theories, increased scepticism about the justification for executive discretion and led to a call for a return to 'fairer' tariff-based sentencing. Rehabilitation, it was argued, was disguised state control, part of the soft state apparatus to ensure conformity. Civil liberties were being infringed because people could be 'treated' (often incarcerated) for an indeterminate period of time and often out of all proportion to the crime committed.

Pragmatists argued that rehabilitation did not work. Martinson (1974:49) concluded that empirical evidence 'gives us very little reason to hope that we have in fact found a sure way of reducing recidivism through rehabilitation' (though one is no longer allowed to use this quotation without pointing out Martinson's later retraction in 1979 – see Raynor, Smith and Vanstone 1994). There were at least two damning pieces of research (Folkard, Smith and Smith 1976; Phillpotts and Lancucki 1979) which purported to demonstrate that offenders given intensive supervision did no better than those given ordinary or no supervision and in some cases did worse. Others argued from a symbolic interactionist perspective that intensive intervention could do more harm than good by labelling offenders and amplifying their deviance, making it more likely that they would react by reoffending.

At the same time, the ideology of the New Right sought to buttress individualism, familialism and nationalism by encouraging the stigmatisation of 'outgroups' and emphasising the need for social discipline (Walker and Beaumont 1985). Right-wing critics argued that rehabilitation was soft and that what offenders needed was greater control and surveillance. They appealed to 'common sense' arguments that if offenders were to be kept out of prison then the alternatives had to be tough and demanding. The Criminal Justice Act 1972 introduced community service orders which involved probation officers in supervising offenders undertaking unpaid (often manual) work, with little obvious social work content in the relationship. It proved a popular sentence with courts and resulted in a dramatic decline in the use of probation orders.

With the tide of national politics turning towards an explicit 'law and order' agenda the probation service was obliged to revise its approach to offenders or risk the kind of swingeing financial cuts which Social Services experienced in the late 1970s. The changing role of the service will be discussed in more detail in Chapter 5 but these attacks left it unsure of its foundation and the issue of 'care versus control' came to dominate professional thinking in the early 1980s.

With the new Conservative government in 1979 began a fundamental review of the identity and ethos of the service. At one end of the spectrum, Haxby (1978) advocated the creation of a 'community correctional service', with the emphasis on punishment and strict 'alternatives to custody'. Other writers sought ways of reconciling the increasingly conflicting demands to care and control, the most influential being an article by Bottoms and McWilliams (1979) entitled 'A non-treatment paradigm for probation practice' which recommended abandoning the medical model of probation (based on notions of diagnosis, followed by treatment, leading to cure) and replacing it with the language of help, shared assessment and task-centred work. At the other end of the political spectrum, Walker and Beaumont (1981) advocated a radical socialist approach to probation work, emphasising the role of capitalism, poverty and oppression in the perpetuation of crime. The views of the latter were widely embraced within the National Association of Probation Officers, the professional association and trade union for probation officers.

⨍ Alongside the developments in professional thinking based on broad political and criminological ideas came the rise of managerialism and accountability in the Thatcherite 1980s. Under the umbrella of the Financial Management Initiative which emphasised economy, efficiency and effectiveness, the Home Office, which had previously adopted a *laissez-faire* attitude to the 55 probation areas, decided to reassert its control. In 1984 the Home Office formulated its *Statement of National Objectives and Priorities*, which, according to Beaumont, established priorities 'by rationing resources between existing activities, rather than prioritising desirable improvements' (1995:53). During 1985 and 1986 probation areas responded with their own *Statements of Local Objectives and Priorities* and, in an attempt to forestall further central government interference, engaged the services of financial management consultants. The implications of these developments for the role of the probation officer will be examined in more detail in Chapter 5. At this point, it is sufficient to point out that such developments had the effect of further undermining the notion of the probation officer as a 'caseworker', whose main professional skills lay in establishing helping relationships with individual offenders.

Meanwhile, a parallel and complementary debate was taking place over the role of Social Services Departments in relation to juvenile delinquents. The history and development of this debate will be examined fully in Chapter 10 but it is important to note here that, following the ill-fated 'short, sharp shock' experiment at New Hall and Send Detention Centres in 1980 and the unprecedentedly high level of the Youth Custody Centre population (7,700 in 1981), there was genuine concern about overcrowding in the youth custody system.

The 1982 Criminal Justice Act introduced criteria which courts had to be satisfied were met before sending a young offender to custody, and in 1983 the Home Secretary announced a new initiative to provide alternatives to custody for more serious and persistent young offenders. The Intermediate Treatment initiative launched by Local Authority Circular LAC 3/83 saw some £15 million invested in over 100 projects around the country. This, together with the increased use of police cautioning for minor offences led to a dramatic reduction in the numbers of juveniles both entering the formal criminal justice system and being sent to custody. By 1990 fewer than 2,000 juveniles were being imprisoned annually.

But, as we shall see later, underlying this trend was a conscious move by juvenile justice social workers away from intervention which focused on the welfare of the child and towards a policy of minimal intervention designed to manage both the decisions made by the criminal justice system (systems management) and the criminal career of the juvenile (the alternative tariff approach) (Pitts 1992a)

The decarceration debate

During this period, the various critiques of rehabilitation tended to confuse institutional rehabilitative approaches with non-incarcerative rehabilitative approaches. The argument for decarceration was based on the realisation that prisons (and, indeed, other institutions) were wholly inappropriate environments in which to attempt to reform deviant behaviour. But such arguments begged two questions. First, is this the only (or even the main) reason for supporting decarceration? Second, what is the nature of 'rehabilitation' outside the institution? It was to these questions that four particular writers – Andrew Scull, Stanley Cohen, Thomas Mathiesen and Anthony Bottoms – addressed themselves in the early 1980s.

Identifying the gap between the rhetoric and the reality of deinstitutionalisation, Scull (1977/1984) launched a scathing attack on those who advocated community treatment for mentally ill and criminal deviants. Isn't it miraculous, he asks, with feigned incredulity, that such programmes are not only more humane and effective, but also cheaper than institutional treatment? In a thesis which remains painfully relevant in relation to mentally ill people (but not, as we shall see, in relation to criminals), he argued that decarceration amounted to benign neglect as a consequence of under-resourcing and sheer lack of interest:

Much of the time, it appears as if the policy makers simply do not know what will happen when their schemes are put into effect. Nor do they seem very concerned to find out. Often, they do not even know where those they have dumped back on the rest of us are to be found.   (Scull 1984:1)

In summary, then, Scull's concern was that decarceration would fail to provide mentally ill people and criminals with the care and supervision they require and thus render both them and the community vulnerable to danger and unacceptable behaviour. One of the consequences of this would be an increase in moral panics among the non-deviant community and a backlash of rejection and practices of exclusion which would be every bit as stigmatising and non-rehabilitative as institutionalisation had been.

The problem with Scull's thesis, however, was that he chose to build on Goffman's previous work on 'total institutions' (Goffman 1961), which had argued that there were certain characteristics which were common to many institutions (the asylum and the prison being among the most notable) and which resulted in the institutionalisation of inmates. Scull mistakenly believed, therefore, that the deinstitutionalisation of mental patients and criminals could also be subjected to an identical analysis.

But while mental hospitals were emptying and closing down, prisons were not. On the contrary, prison building was expanding and the prison population constantly rising. At the same time as the Home Secretary (then Leon Brittan) was attempting to regain centralised control over the probation service and arguably raise its profile as a credible provider of alternatives to custody, he was also announcing the largest prison-building programme ever. Far from seeing the convicted felon's chance of receiving a prison sentence grow ever more remote (Scull 1977/1984), it was clear that alternatives to custody were rapidly becoming no more than supplements to custody. And far from being supervised by probation officers 'with caseloads of one and two hundred persons' (Scull 1977/1984:2), criminals were being subjected to a matrix of ever more complex social-control mechanisms in the name of community corrections. The argument that community corrections are undoubtedly cheaper than prisons was, and remains, fairly irrelevant. The fact is that people are prepared to pay for the punishment of criminals; they are not prepared to pay for their treatment. Community corrections will attract resources if they are dressed up as punishment but they will fail to attract even modest resources if they are perceived only as treatment.

Cohen's critique of decarceration (1979, 1983, 1985) owed more to Foucault's concept of the 'dispersal of discipline' than to Goffman's concept of the 'total institution'. His analysis of the history of 'social control talk' juxtaposed three different rhetorics, which made Scull's analysis appear simplistic. Accepting that, in an imperfect world, progress will never be unimpeded, Cohen describes, first, an optimistic conservative rhetoric which argues that penal reform has been steady and that decarceration represents the enlightened values of an ever more civilised society. By contrast, Cohen's second account of penal change reflects the liberal disillusion with rehabilitation which characterised much of the symbolic interactionist literature on the sociology of deviance and the 'nothing works' approach to punishment. Rather than seeking reform, we should be looking for ways to manage – both the system and individual criminal careers – so as to cause the least damage, cost and inconvenience to the rest of society. But Cohen's third model presents a conspiracy of the powerful to mystify and obfuscate:

Humanism, good intentions, professional knowledge and reform rhetoric are neither in the idealist sense the producers of change, nor in the materialist sense the mere products of changes in the political economy ... [T]he exercise of power itself creates and causes to emerge new objects of knowledge and accumulates new bodies of information. (Cohen 1983:107)

The decarcerated criminal is one such new object of knowledge about whom new bodies of information must be accumulated. Community programmes, far from reducing the restrictions on criminals who might otherwise have been sent to prison, create a new clientèle of criminals who are controlled or disciplined by other mechanisms. The boundaries between freedom and confinement become blurred. The 'net' of social control is thus thrown ever wider into the community, its thinner mesh designed to trap ever smaller 'fish'. Once caught in the net, the penetration of disciplinary intervention is ever deeper, reaching every aspect of the criminal's life.

The particular insight which Thomas Mathiesen adds to Cohen's analysis is a prediction that the future of social control will involve a move away from the identification and punishment of individuals towards the criminalisation of 'whole groups and categories – through planned manipulation . . . of the everyday life conditions of these groups and categories' (1983:139). From the growth of private security and CCTV to the 1994 legislation against travellers and proposals to place a curfew on all children under ten (*Independent*, 3 June 1996), it is not difficult to find examples of the fulfilment of Mathiesen's prophecy.

The appeal of such radical critiques is undeniable. The spectre of George Orwell's *Nineteen Eighty Four* (1949) produces a frisson of resistance in most of us but the mundane reality of criminal justice is less spectacular or threatening. Most punishment, Anthony Bottoms (1983) argues, is not about the creation of docile bodies but the more routine business of disqualification from – and subsequent requalification to – full citizenship. Most offences are dealt with by means of monetary penalties – fines or compensation – and other disposals which do not involve supervision. The purpose is intentionally and openly to penalise unacceptable actions, to prevent repetition and to deter others by making examples of those who infringe the rules. There is nothing particularly sinister about the process and there is no congruence 'with a general thesis of a thrust towards indefinite discipline' (Bottoms 1983:178). We must be as careful not to be carried away by moral panics about punishment as we are to resist moral panics about crime itself.

Enter discourse analysis

At this point, it is necessary to introduce some of the conceptual tools of discourse analysis in order to make sense of the paradoxical and inconsistent developments in both academic and policy thinking in the early years of the 1980s. Discourse analysis is concerned with the relationship between power and the production of knowledge (Worrall 1990/1995). It is concerned with all aspects of a communication – not only its content, but its author (who says it?), its authority (on what grounds?) its audience (to whom?), its object (about whom?) and its objective (in order to achieve what?) What are the mechanisms whereby, in the face of a fragmented and contradictory reality, claims to know can be successfully translated into effective unified knowledge with over-determined consequences?

First, that reality has to be reconstructed as a field of recognisable (that is, unified and ideologically congruent) objects in which it is possible to intervene on the basis of prior existing knowledge. The observable phenomenon of people breaking the law has to be programmed as people who break the law and about whom knowledge already exists, has always existed, and is waiting to be laid claim to. And that knowledge already contains within it (perversely hidden but ultimately reachable) its own inevitable consequences and 'correct' solutions (Worrall 1990/ 1995).

The fragmented and contradictory reality of 'alternatives to custody' consists, *inter alia*, of the following elements:

- a consensus that prison can never be a genuine site of rehabilitation and that some attempt must be made to keep those criminals deemed capable of being rehabilitated out of prison;
- a lack of consensus about the effectiveness of non-incarcerative rehabilitation and a concern about the effects (whether intended or unintended) of measures which blur the boundaries between prison and freedom;
- a political decision to expand, rather than reduce, the number of places available in prison, thereby removing some of the pressure from sentencers to utilise alternatives to custody; and
- consequent political pressure on the probation service to compete for its clientèle either by proving its rehabilitative effectiveness or by demonstrating that supervision can serve other punitive purposes (such as surveillance and monitoring) which supplement prison but do so at far less cost.

Second, the programme of finding the 'correct' solution to the problem of 'people who break the law' requires a channel of conveyance. The *technology* of such conveyance is varied and disparate. It may consist of architectural institutions, like courtrooms, prisons or probation centres; it may consist of practices such as the provision of welfare, the ascription of motives or practices of exclusion. Finally, it may consist of norms – technologies which have been internalised to the extent that they are no longer recognised as technologies at all. Self-regulation demonstrates the supreme success of a programme (Worrall 1990/1995). An example of a practice of exclusion crucial to the conveyance of the programme of Punishment in the Community is the ejection from the discourse of rehabilitation of any legitimate concern for the welfare of the criminal. Instead, that concern is constructed as Other – the non-legitimated account of lived experience which threatens, and must be controlled by, the programme. The personal or social welfare of the criminal is explicitly detached from, and made discursively irrelevant to, the process of preventing recidivism. Offending is a matter of choice, not something determined by circumstances, and modern rehabilitation 'addresses offending behaviour' – it is not concerned with the offender's address (see Chapter 6).

Third, programmes and technologies are dependent for their success on *strategies* of intervention (Worrall 1990/1995). Strategy is not the coherent, logical, overall planning of action (although it may be represented as such). Rather, it is an opportunistic and expedient means of exploiting the field of intervention. It is the means whereby the authority of programmes can be maintained (or denied) in spite of (and yet because of) their effects. Strategy is the process whereby individuals and agencies attempt to anticipate the effects of programmes and technologies and then utilise those effects to justify the continuation or cessation of such intervention. It is the means by which a programme 'caters in advance for the eventuality of its own failure' (Gordon 1979:38). The tenacity of electronic monitoring, discussed below, is an excellent example of strategy.

The discussion which follows deconstructs the representation of Punishment in the Community as a coherent framework of response to crime and attempts to expose the absence of that which is represented as being present: namely, the political will to send fewer criminals to prison.

Greenpapering over the cracks

The process began with a strategy of consultation through the publication in 1988 of the Green Paper, *Punishment, Custody and the Community* (Home Office 1988). Responding to the rapidly increasing prison population which threatened to outgrow even the ambitious new prison-building programme, the government stated quite clearly that

Imprisonment is not the most effective punishment for most crime. Custody should be reserved as punishment for very serious offences . . .

(Home Office 1988:2)

Within these two short phrases can be found the two crucial words which not only formed the foundation of the Criminal Justice Act, but which simultaneously constituted the 'cracks' in that foundation – 'punishment' and 'serious'. It will be argued in Chapter 3 that it was the reliance on the ill-defined concept of 'offence seriousness' that brought about the demise of the 1991 Act. For the moment the focus will remain on the use of the term 'punishment' in official criminal justice discourse from the time of the publication of the Green Paper.

In a speech to the Annual Conference of the Association of Chief Officers of Probation (ACOP) in September 1988, John Patten (then Home Office Minister of State) attempted to define 'punishment' in such a way as to make it palatable to a professional group which, while accepting that its work included elements of control, had traditionally found it difficult to incorporate the word 'punishment' into its vocabulary. Patten's argument will be quoted in full because its logic is central to the theme of this book:

I acknowledge straight away that there is an inherent tension between the concept of control – let alone punishment – and the roles of the probation service which are variously described as 'welfare', 'caring' or 'helping' . . . But I still use the word 'punishment'. My reason for this lies in some basic truths about the way the criminal justice system operates and how the public perceive it. Taking the public first, their concept of punishment, I suggest, is that of an offender being subject to restrictions on liberty, inconvenience and even to financial penalties; these restrictions to be proportionate to the degree of inconvenience the offender has caused for society or for his [*sic*] victims. They will be reflected in restrictions on his ability to do what he wants and when, and in the obligations which are put on him to face the reasons for his offending, the consequences for his victim and the need for reparation to society. The Green Paper recognises that in some cases the perception of punishment can be met only by a custodial sentence. It argues, however, that it would be adequately met in case of significant other categories of offenders, by . . . punishment in the community. *The fact is that all probation-based disposals are already in varying degrees forms of punishment. For example, the offender who has to report to a probation officer, or work specified hours on CS or spend 60 days at a day centre is clearly being punished. It is bizarre to scratch around to find polite euphemisms for what is going on.*　　　　(Patten 1988:12, original emphasis)

At one level, the logic of this argument is flawed. Whether one is reading the work of a radical writer like Foucault (1977) or a conventional criminologist like Walker (1991), no one pretends that the only definition of 'punishment' is the narrow one of incarceration of or inflicting pain on the physical body. According to Walker, punishment 'involves the infliction of something which is assumed to be unwelcome to the recipient' (1991:1). The infliction has to be intentional (deliberate) and for a reason (the breaking of a law) – accidental harm does not count. Nevertheless, no one would dispute that a conditional discharge or a fine are, *in a sense*, punishments, as are probation orders and community service orders, in so far as they are unwelcome inconveniences.

But what this technical definition fails to address is the purpose of punishment and it is here that Patten's definition so clearly (but implicitly) parts company from the traditional value base of the probation service. It is one thing to say that punishment is an inevitable (even desirable) by-product of placing an offender on probation. It is quite another to say that punishment is the purpose of such an order. On the surface, Patten is arguing for the 'just deserts' philosophy which became explicit in the later White Paper – the imposition of proportionate restriction of liberty or inconvenience. But underneath is an attempt to appropriate a range of other, different, principles (deterrence, reform, rehabilitation) and to argue that they can be subsumed within a 'just deserts' discourse, because they are not incompatible with it.

What is being presented here is a falsely constructed politics of consensus. Instead of acknowledging genuine conflicts of interest and philosophy and arguing for a pragmatic compromise, the argument is presented in such a way as to pretend that *there is no conflict*, except in the minds of dangerously inflexible subversives, who apparently delight in the 'bizarre' practice of 'scratch(ing) around to find polite euphemisms'.

So one of the ways in which the government sought to greenpaper over the cracks of a penal crisis which was threatening to run out of control because of the lack of accountability of sentencers (Parker 1988) was to argue that 'we're all in the business of punishment'. There are no differences of principle, only differences of approach and language – and credibility. It is not, so the argument goes, that the government is opposed to non-custodial disposals. On the contrary, it wishes to enhance their status and extend their use by introducing the possibility of 'mixing and matching', to enable sentencers to make their own unique 'designer packages'. Apart from anything else, 'punishment in the community should be more economical in public resources' (Home Office 1988:2). But in order to do this, it has to be recognised that 'not every sentencer or member of the public had full confidence in the present orders which leave offenders in the community' (Home Office 1988:2). In other words, responsibility for making the new packages work lies not with sentencers but with those who provide what must now be referred to as 'tough and demanding punishment' for people who must no longer be called 'clients' but must now be referred to as 'offenders'. As John Patten rightly says, 'this is more than a semantic point' (Patten, 1988:11).

A fate worse than prison?

The Green Paper made the fundamental mistake of assuming that offenders would (and could) do virtually anything in order to avoid a prison sentence. The later White Paper recognised that much crime was not committed after careful calculation of the possible gains and risks:

> Much crime is committed on impulse . . . by offenders who live from moment to moment; their crimes are as impulsive as the rest of their feckless, sad or pathetic lives. It is unrealistic to construct sentencing arrangements on the assumption that most offenders will weigh up the possibilities in advance and base their conduct on rational calculation. Often they do not.
>
> (Home Office 1990a:2.8)

But that eloquent insight was something for the future. In 1988, the government believed that it could make non-custodial sentencing almost as complicated and demanding as it wished. Admittedly, there was some acknowledgement that sentences had to be 'realistic':

> If the requirements are made too demanding, it is more likely that the offender will fail to complete it satisfactorily and this could result in his imprisonment. This would defeat the purpose of the order.   (Home Office 1988:14)

Despite this, the Green Paper goes on to suggest, as an example, that an offender in full-time employment or education could, nevertheless, be given an order which included a daily curfew, weekly community service, tracking (daily contact with a supervisor), paying compensation and having regular interviews with a probation officer to discuss his offending behaviour. For an unemployed offender, the package would include two days community service, two days at a day centre and two days 'prescribed activity' in addition to the daily curfew. It was this proposed punitive overload that prompted Pat Carlen to raise the question of sentence *feasibility* and the obligation that should be placed on sentencers 'in the cases of offenders bearing multiple social disadvantage [to] attempt to do least harm by making non-punitive and totally supportive orders' (Carlen 1990a:120).

In the event, the proposed 'supervision and restriction order' did not materialise but the Green Paper did succeed in bringing about another highly restrictive measure, that of electronic monitoring. Tagging could not be used on sentenced offenders without specific legislation, but there was nothing to stop courts experimenting with it as a condition of bail. Again, the assumption was that offenders would put up with anything rather be remanded in custody. Indeed, Tom Stacey (founder of the incredibly named Offenders' Tag Association) argued strongly that opposition to tagging was based on 'wilful ignorance' of the appalling nature of prison conditions and the 'vested interests' of the civil libertarian and penal reform lobbies. As well as wishing to avoid prison, offenders, he argues, would also prefer to be tagged than have to talk to a probation officer! (Stacey 1989). Leaving aside Mike Nellis' persuasive reply that tagging (by private security companies) is an 'effective means of control over the dispossessed communities – the underclass – who are surplus to capitalism's requirements' (Nellis 1989), it soon became clear in the three experimental schemes that, for some offenders at least, electronic monitoring was a fate worse than prison. Christopher Varney is reported to have asked a judge to return him to prison because he did not like the 'flea-ridden' hostel where he was ordered to live under curfew (*Guardian*, 29 November 1989). But the best-documented story is that of Richard Hart, aged 23, who was the first person to be allowed to stay at home subject to curfew restrictions monitored by an electronic anklet.

Richard Hart was accused of taking a car without consent and stealing a cashcard. He had been on remand in custody for eight weeks but his wife had a baby during that time and the magistrates decided to grant him bail to care for his wife and three-day-old daughter. Unfortunately, however, Hart did not have a telephone, so the court had to arrange for one to be installed before the monitoring equipment could be used (*Guardian*, 18 August 1989). A week later, it was reported that the Hart family was woken up by the police in the middle of the night because the ankle-tag and transmitter were malfunctioning and falsely indicating that he was breaking his bail conditions. But . . .

Losing a night's sleep is proving the least of unemployed Mr Hart's problems. It was bad enough that he is not allowed to move more than 200 feet from his telephone for 21 hours a day, but the Department of Social Security has ruled that he is not available for work and cannot claim benefit . . . The family is living on 60 per cent of the discretionary hardship grant of £24.90 a week.

(*Guardian*, 23 August, 1989)

When he was first tagged, Hart had said 'Agreeing to being tagged was not an easy decision to make, because it could be like being a prisoner in my own home.' (*Guardian*, August 18 1989). By November, Hart appears to have decided that there was a price that was too high to pay for freedom. With his solicitor complaining that his monitoring equipment had malfunctioned 15 times since it was fitted, Hart was returned to custody for 'alleged breaches of bail conditions' (*Guardian*, 29 November 1989).

According to the Prison Reform Trust (1990a), by January 1990, only 46 defendants had been tagged on contracts which cost the taxpayer £564,706. Of these, 24 had breached the conditions of their bail, been arrested for further offences, or absconded. As we shall see in the next chapter, the attempt by the 1994 Criminal Justice and Public Order Act to revive the fortunes of electronic monitoring has been no more successful in terms of numbers and considerably more expensive. We should not be surprised. Electronic monitoring is an idea we have copied wholesale from America and, as Whitfield explains, 'the main message is that electronic monitoring in the USA is a shambles' (1995:19). He suggests four factors which contributed to its inappropriate expansion: aggressive marketing by vendors; the promise that it would 'do something' about prison overcrowding; a belief that it might cost less than imprisonment; and a naïve and totally unrealistic expectation of what the technology could achieve.

Crime, Justice and Protecting the Public

Following this period of 'consultation', the White Paper *Crime, Justice and Protecting the Public* (Cmnd. 965, Home Office 1990a) set out the government's proposals for 'better justice through a more consistent approach to sentencing, so that convicted criminals get their "just desserts" ' [*sic*] (1990a:2), though its public reception was not assisted by the persistent typographical error that invited jokes about porridge and prison puddings!

Joking aside, the shift in policy represented by the White Paper was hailed by the then Home Secretary, David Waddington, as heralding 'the most fundamental and far-reaching changes for at least half a century in the way offenders were punished' (*The Times*, 6 February 1990). Elsewhere it was suggested that the proposals 'will come to be compared to the introduction of the probation service in 1907 and the Labour government's abandonment of flogging in 1948' (*Independent*, 7 February 1990). The White Paper had a mixed reception and there was a recognition that the government was making a 'brave gamble . . . a strange compromise, attempting to achieve real penal reform while appeasing judges and the law-and-order lobby' (*Independent*, 7 February 1990). A prophetic warning was given that the policy could 'backfire if sentencers failed to impose the new community-based penalties' (*The Times*, 7 February 1990). Nevertheless, commenting with the advantage of hindsight, the policies underpinning the Criminal Justice Act 1991 were very carefully considered and now look remarkably liberal for a Conservative government that had been in power for 12 years. As David Faulkner has since said:

these policies had evolved gradually, through a process which took account of public feeling but which was largely driven by consultation with professionals, practitioners, academics and representatives of informed opinion . . . there was a sense of continuity over quite long periods of time.

(*Guardian*, 11 November 1993)

[Professional groups greeted the proposals with a mixture of caution, scepticism and optimism. Some (such as NAPO) saw a dominant emphasis on retributivist punishment, indicating a fundamental change in the role and nature of the probation service, marking its end as a social-work agency. Others (such as the Prison Reform Trust) welcomed the underlying principle of reducing the prison population but regretted the continued wide discretion to be allowed to sentencers and the absence of concern about the needs of offenders. The probation service itself, however, seemed to accept that behind its tough language, the White Paper proposals were extremely pragmatic. They heralded an expanded role for the service, with more report-writing, more supervision and more prison aftercare (and, it was hoped, more resources). If the service was prepared to concede the language of punishment, then it seemed that it would be allowed, by and large, to get on with the job it wanted to do.]

Conclusion

The decade of the 1980s saw the gradual convergence of political, professional and academic discourses whose origins, authors and desires (or aims) differed widely. The broad sociological debates about decarceration and the demise of the rehabilitative ideal became elided with professional debates about managerialism and the political imperative for the Conservative government to be seen to be *successful* in controlling crime. For a brief moment in political history, there was a consensus that the best way to demonstrate success might be to reduce, rather than increase, the number of people being sent to prison. But, as with other such moments (notably the 1969 Children and Young Person Act – see Chapter 10), by the time the consensus was set in the 'stone tablets' of legislation, the tide of public opinion was already turning. Reducing the prison population was soon to be seen as a sign of weakness, rather than strength, in the battle against crime.

CHAPTER 3

The Criminal Justice Act 1991 and its demise

So here we go again, on the punishment train with yet more trucks being coupled . . . on to an already overburdened and lengthy express, hurtling nowhere quickly, with an inexhaustible power supply and seemingly infinite capacity to collect, reprocess and dump its perceived 'human waste' with little thought about the personal, social and environmental costs.   (Broad 1991:22)

Introduction

The Criminal Justice Act 1991 came into force in October 1992 and was the first major review of criminal justice legislation since 1982. It aimed to provide a new coherent sentencing framework based on the principle of just deserts with only the most serious of offences being punished with imprisonment. Less serious offences were to be dealt with by means of three other categories of disposals: discharges (for the bulk of minor offences), financial penalties and community sentences.

The background to the Act was a growing concern with overcrowding in prisons and a related belief that alternative, non-custodial sentences were viewed by sentencers as being 'soft options'. It was accepted that some offenders were being sent to prison unnecessarily and some were being sent for too long. The Woolf Report into the prison disturbances of April 1990 (Woolf and Tumim 1991) and the Reed Report (Department of Health/Home Office 1992) into the treatment of mentally disordered offenders had both highlighted the dangers of inappropriate custodial sentences and of prison overcrowding. Attention was increasingly being paid to adopting appropriate criteria for custody, especially in the Juvenile Court. There was also a recognition that sentencing lacked consistency and that this in itself was unjust. Evidence was growing that black people and women might be experiencing discrimination in the courts. Finally, there was dissatisfaction that courts appeared to make insufficient distinction between violent and sexual offences against the person and offences against property.

Key principles of the Act

The Act was based on six key principles (Sanders and Senior 1994):

1 *Sentences should reflect the seriousness of the offences committed (otherwise known as proportionality) and custody should be reserved for only the most serious offences* (1994:124).

The Act required a court to focus primarily on the seriousness of the offence before it and to send the defendant to prison only if that offence and, if appropriate, one other associated offence were so serious that only such a sentence could be justified (section 1). This was intended to prevent courts from sending someone to prison for a number of minor offences, none of which in itself warranted imprisonment.

The Act also prevented courts from giving too much consideration to previous convictions, unless the circumstances of those offences should shed light on (or 'disclose') features of the current offence which make it more serious (section 29). This section was intended to restrict the powers of a court to send someone to prison for repeatedly committing minor offences.

2 *A sharper distinction should be drawn between property offences and offences against the person* (1994:124).

This reflects the government's concern that people committing violent and sexual offences should be dealt with particularly severely. To this end, courts were permitted to consider the need to protect the public from serious harm when deciding the length of prison sentences for these offences.

3 *Community sentences stand in their own right and should not be seen as alternatives to custody* (1994:125).

This principle refuted the popular misbelief of the 1980s that most offenders deserved to go to prison and that if they were given a non-custodial sentence, they were being 'let off' with a 'soft' alternative. The Act recognised that community sentences (that is, probation and supervision orders, curfew orders, community service orders, combination orders and attendance centre orders) constituted a sentencing band in their own right, providing a particular degree of restriction on liberty commensurate with a particular level of offence seriousness.

4 *Young people should be dealt with in a way that takes account of their maturity and stage of development* (1994:125).

The Act replaced the Juvenile Court (which dealt with offenders aged 10–16) with the Youth Court (which deals with offenders aged 10–17). At the same time, however, it allowed courts to impose certain adult sentences (probation order, community service order, combination order) on 16- and 17-year-olds. This meant that courts could treat 16- and 17-year-olds as either juveniles or adults, depending on their maturity and stage of development. Very little guidance was given to courts to help them define and assess maturity objectively and there was some concern that the concept could result in prejudiced judgements of teenagers' circumstances and abilities.

5 *The intention of the court should be properly reflected in the way that a prison sentence is served* (1994:125).

The Act introduced a clearly defined system of early release for prisoners which replaced the much-criticised parole system. Put simply, the Act abolished automatic remission after two-thirds of the sentence and discretionary parole after one-third (or six months, whichever is the longer). Instead it provided that half of all sentences must be served in custody. Thereafter, there was a system of automatic release (with or without licence conditions) during which time a prisoner may be recalled to prison if they reoffend. Parole remained an option only for long-term prisoners.

6   *The whole criminal justice system should be administered efficiently and without discrimination* (1994:126).

The Act contained a significant new provision (section 95) for monitoring the criminal justice system to ensure 'value for money' and the absence of discrimination on the ground of race or sex or any other improper ground. To these ends, the Secretary of State was required to publish relevant information annually. Cynics have pointed out the incongruous coupling of discrimination issues with concerns about financial implications.

The Act made two further major changes, one of which was later revoked. The introduction of *unit fines* was intended to force courts to give systematic consideration to offenders' means when imposing fines, recognising that the same fine could be insignificant for a rich person while causing devastating hardship for a poor one.

The Act also replaced the *Social Inquiry Reports* (SIRs) prepared by the probation service with *Pre-sentence Reports* (PSRs). Such reports provide courts with information about the offender to assist in sentencing but, while SIRs focused primarily on social and personal information relating to the offender's welfare, PSRs were required to focus more clearly on the offence and to include only information which was relevant to it. Probation officers were also no longer allowed to make professional sentencing recommendations, but must instead discuss proposals for suitable options, making clear that the final decision rests with the court (as it always has).

Criticisms of the Act and amendments to it

The Criminal Justice Act 1991 represented the culmination of Thatcherite criminal justice policy and was surprisingly radical in its attempt to implement a 'just deserts' model of sentencing, which endorsed community penalties for the vast majority of offenders. Within six months, however, the key concepts of the Act had come under such vociferous attack that they were revoked. Yet the 1993 amendments were constructed within official discourse as being no more than a 'review'. According to a former deputy secretary at the Home Office in charge of criminal justice policy until 1992, there is now a serious void at the centre of the criminal justice system. There is no clearly understood set of purposes which it is meant to achieve or principles which it is meant to observe, and no effective and acceptable system of accountability for its operation.   (Faulkner, *Guardian*, 11 November 1993)

The whole point of the 1991 Act was to reduce the prison population by decentring the prison from penal discourse. This was done in four ways: first, by focusing on the seriousness of the offence and limiting the extent to which previous convictions could be taken into account; second, by raising the status of community punishment; third, by making financial penalties fairer so that fewer people would go to prison for non-payment; and fourth, by explicitly outlawing discrimination and thus aiming to reduce the disproportionate number of black people in prison and the inappropriate use of prison for women.

The Act appeared to be very successful initially in achieving its objectives. Home Office Statistical Bulletin 25/93 indicated a fall in the proportionate use of immediate custody, especially among offenders with numerous previous convictions, a rise in the proportionate use of the fine (with average fines increasing for those in employment and decreasing for the unemployed) and a rise in the proportionate use of community sentences.

Within six months of its implementation, however, it was being described as a shambles. Three aspects in particular were claimed by sentencers to be unworkable:

1 The 'two offence rule', contained in section 1(2)(a), which required courts to consider only the offence and one other associated with it when deciding on a custodial sentence;
2 The admittedly obscurely drafted section 29 which had placed restrictions on the consideration of previous convictions; and
3 The use of unit fines.

By August 1993, all three had been abolished, thus effectively reversing the whole ethos of the original Act. Section 66 of the 1993 Criminal Justice Act allowed courts, when deciding on a custodial sentence, to consider 'the totality of the offending behaviour' with which it is dealing (Magistrates' Association 1993). Courts were also allowed to take into account any previous convictions and any failure to respond to previous sentences. Finally, section 65 of the 1993 Act blandly required courts to inquire into the financial circumstances of the offender before imposing a fine.

The fall of the unit fine

There is no reason why the principle of unit fines (systematically relating fines to means as well as offence seriousness) should not have been acceptable in England and Wales. Similar approaches have been used in many other European countries and in parts of America (Tonry and Hamilton 1995). Experiments in English and Welsh courts indicated that the idea was feasible and an improvement on the previous system. It seemed that courts were happy to reduce fines for poorer people and that the fines were consequently paid more quickly, with less default and, therefore, fewer imprisonments for non-payment. With hindsight, there was perhaps insufficient attention paid to sentencers' reluctance to increase fines for richer offenders and this became one subsequent explanation for the downfall of unit fines. Old attitudes of charitable munificence towards the poor (which accounted for the initial welcome of unit fines) were misinterpreted by policy-makers as a willingness to embrace the principles of 'equality of impact' implied by unit fines.

There were undoubtedly some technical difficulties in deciding the minimum and maximum sums to be attached to units (Moxon 1995). In the experiments, the maximum had been about £20 per unit but the 1991 Act increased this to £100. This resulted in some anomalously large fines for only moderately well-off offenders committing minor offences. This was exacerbated by the discretion given to sentencers when offenders (particularly those who pleaded guilty by post) failed to provide proper information about their means. In theory, sentencers could then impose whatever fine they thought reasonable but some (perhaps to make the point) chose to impose the maximum. Inevitably, mistakes (possibly wilful) occurred. In one case, a motorist decided to go to court to defend himself against a fixed penalty for illegal parking and was fined £500. In another, an unemployed man was fined £1200 for throwing a crisp packet on the ground. In both cases the offender had failed to provide correct means information and in both cases the fine was properly reduced on appeal. Yet a few celebrated cases of 'unfairness' such as these were apparently all that was needed to abandon the venture.

Central to the downfall of unit fines was the perception of sentencers that their discretion in these matters was being eroded (Baker 1993). According to Baker, magistrates felt that the old system had worked well, that they had not been consulted about the new system and that it created insuperable problems. They found difficulty in 'thinking in units' and remained wedded to the notion of 'set worth':

The magistrates saw certain crimes as being worth certain amounts of money . . . they cannot be seen as more serious if one offender commits them than another. If double parking is worth £100, then it is worth £100, regardless of how much you earn.   (Baker 1993:68)

A few magistrates actually resigned because they felt they were being forced to adhere to rigid rules which resulted in unfair penalties. This much could surely have been anticipated and tolerated as 'teething problems'. That the whole system should be abandoned in less than a year suggests a studied lack of political will.

Swarming circumstances[1]

So, was the whole Punishment in the Community era an aberration, merely a stop-gap measure or worse – a deliberate conspiracy to prove that liberalism must fail? The Hurd vision demonstrated a willingness by at least some members of the government to engage in Garland's rationalisation of punishment (1990) but it could never eradicate the constant conflict, tension and compromise that has always characterised penal history. As Garland reminds us, conflicts exist between ideological ambitions and financial constraints, between political expediency and established sensibilities, between the requirements of security and those of morality, between the interests of different professional groups. And 'these swarming circumstances are only ever resolved into particular outcomes by means of . . . struggles, negotiations, actions and decisions' (1990:285) which involve compromise and sacrifice.

The failure of the 1991 Criminal Justice Act was not due to its inability to achieve its objective of decentring the prison – it was initially very successful in doing that – but to its inability to establish the 'punitive city' outside the prison. Despite, or perhaps because of, the fear of an Orwellian society, there is a great deal of resistance to any discourse which appears to 'blur the boundaries' and widen or strengthen the net of social control. Garland described a 'paranoid culture', indicating that 'the relations of the individual to the political community are pathologically out of sorts' (1995:3) So rather than view the rise and fall of the discourse of Punishment in the Community as either a story of 'benevolence gone wrong' or 'mystification'(Cohen 1983), it can be seen as a period of strange and paradoxical but effective refusal or resistance by the courts and the public (but not by probation officers) to accept the programmes, technologies and strategies of power which sought to construct punishment or penality as a continuum of control.

Amid increasing concern about the perceived diminution of the powers of the courts by the 1991 Act, a new moral panic about young offenders gathered steam in 1992 and 1993. The riots of the summer of 1991, which were perceived to be largely the result of confrontation between young men and the police following attempts by the latter to clamp down on 'joyriding' (Campbell 1993), the media construction of 'rat boy' as the epitome of the persistent young offender responsible for a disproportionate amount of crime (Hagell and Newburn 1994) and the appalling murder of James Bulger all contributed to a climate of public anxiety that could only be satisfied by a complete political U-turn. No longer would public opinion tolerate any blurring of the boundary between freedom and confinement. If you commit a crime, you deserve to be excluded from the law-abiding community. Michael Howard's infamous speech at the Conservative Party Conference in Blackpool in October 1993 caught the mood of public opinion brilliantly:

Let us be clear. Prison works. It ensures that we are protected from murderers, muggers and rapists – and it will make many who are tempted to commit crimes think twice.

It is difficult to believe that only months before, the Royal Commission on Criminal Justice (the Runciman Committee) had reported, following the concern about miscarriages of justice that had been highlighted by the release of the Birmingham Six in 1991. Its two main recommendations – to set up an independent Criminal Cases Review Authority to consider allegations of miscarriages of justice, and to retain the suspect's right to silence – seemed out of step with public opinion by the summer of 1993 (although many of its other recommendations, such as ending the right to trial by jury and requiring defendants to disclose any defence prior to trial were criticised by radical lawyers for perpetuating injustices). But of much greater public concern by then was the perceived danger of acquitting the guilty or, at least, their overly lenient treatment.

The event that had finally confirmed the change in public opinion was the abduction and murder in February 1993 of two-year-old James Bulger by two ten-year-old boys, Jon Venables and Robert Thompson. The tragic and appalling event was wholly exceptional and might easily not have been constructed as being 'symptomatic of broader tendencies' in society (Hay 1995: 201). But it was. It became 'a mirror within which collective fears and anxieties [were] reflected and simultaneously a screen upon which they [were] focused' (Hay 1995:200). As we shall see in Chapter 10, the event was taken to mark the end of the presumed and idealised innocence of childhood and the confirmation of the threat of children – *all* children were now potential killers.

The Criminal Justice and Public Order Act 1994

At the 1993 Conservative Party Conference, the Home Secretary announced his 27 pledges in an attempt to mop up all the outstanding problems of criminal justice as he saw them. Somewhere between 17 and 19 of these eventually reached the statute book in the 1994 Criminal Justice and Public Order Act (Morton 1994). The key provisions were:

1 Extension of police powers to stop and search.
2 Extension of police powers to take intimate body samples, enabling the police, among other things, to build a DNA database in relation to sex offenders.
3 Introduction of secure training centres for persistent offenders aged 12–14 years.
4 Extension of the existing powers of courts to detain offenders aged 10–13 years for long periods, to include serious offences other than murder or manslaughter. (In particular, this closes a legal loophole whereby boys under 14 were not considered capable of committing rape.)
5 Demonopolisation of local authority secure accommodation, enabling private and voluntary organisations to make such provision.
6 Restrictions on the granting of bail and the removal of the presumption of bail when an offence is alleged to have been committed while on bail.
7 Provision (against the recommendations of the Royal Commission) to

allow courts to draw 'proper inferences' from a suspect's refusal to answer police questions or give evidence in court.

8 Abolition of corroboration rules in the case of accomplice and children's evidence and in sex offence cases. (The compulsory warning given to juries about the unreliability of the uncorroborated evidence of sex-attack victims had long been seen as offensive and its abolition was one of the few provisions that was widely welcomed by reformers).

9 Revision of the legal definition of rape to include the rape of a man.

10 Abolition of committal procedures in Magistrates' Courts.

11 Creation of a new offence of witness intimidation.

12 Explicit acknowledgement of sentence reduction for guilty pleas (known as plea bargaining).

13 Lifting of restrictions on publishing identification information on young offenders in certain circumstances.

14 Extensive provisions to prevent collective trespass or nuisance on land, aimed primarily at demonstrators, squatters and those attending 'raves'.

15 Extensions of bans on obscene publications, to include video games and other computer-generated pornographic images.

16 Extension of provisions for the contracting out of prison services and prisoner escorts.

17 Authorisation of mandatory drugs-testing in prisons.

Of interest also in relation to the arguments of this book is Schedule 9, which makes the following provisions:

- Extension of the Attorney General's powers of appeal against 'unduly lenient' sentences;
- Removal of the mandatory requirement for courts to obtain pre-sentence reports before passing a custodial sentence or certain community sentences;
- Authorisation for new pilot trials of curfew orders and electronic monitoring. (By April 1996 a total of 65 offenders had been tagged in three pilot schemes, at a cost of £1.6 million, according to the reply to a Parliamentary Question reported by the Howard League magazine, *Criminal Justice*, in August 1996);
- Provision for courts to bind over parents of a young offender to ensure that the child complies with the requirements of a community sentence.

Disparate though its numerous sections may appear, the intended effects of the discourse within which the Act is constructed by the Home Secretary are clear. 'The scales of justice have been tilted too far in favour of the offenders. Victims have had a raw deal. I want to redress that balance' (Home Office Press Release 166/94 cited in Morton 1994:8).

By constructing the relationship between offenders and victims in this stark either/or way, the approval of public opinion is secured. The inclusion of one or two high-profile demands by campaigning groups (for example, abolition of the corroboration warning in rape cases, banning computer-generated pornography and creating a new offence of witness intimidation) distracts attention from the criminalisation of whole new groups of citizens and a return to the highly damaging penal incarceration of naughty children.

'Out go holidays': ejecting the Other of probation

Later in the same press release, the Home Secretary turns his fire on community sentences. 'These measures will mean an end to the approach which offers holidays for offenders,' he says, 'Out go holidays and in come tightly controlled community sentences.'

In March 1995 the government produced a consultation document entitled *Strengthening Punishment in the Community* (Home Office 1995c). Its main proposal was to replace existing non-custodial sentences with a single 'community sentence', the exact content of which would be decided by sentencers to suit the perceived needs and requirements of each individual case. The clearly-stated purpose of the proposal was to increase public confidence in non-custodial penalties; the less clearly stated aim (but one equally obvious to the initiated) was to bring the probation service once and for all under the control of the courts by making the purchaser-provider relationship quite explicit.

The essential proposed change is that the probation service should provide community sentences which the courts consider to be required for individual offenders, rather than the courts having to select from the restricted range of sentences which the probation service is able to offer.   (1.4)

Much of the consultation document harks back to the 1988 Green Paper but its tone is one of weariness rather than innovation. If the Green Paper began a new debate then the later consultation document gave every indication of sounding its death knoll. It marked a final disingenuous gesture towards the preservation of the probation service as we know it. 'This is your last chance' is the phrase that seemed to leap from every page. Yet, simultaneously, opposition was anticipated and, with it, the perfect excuse to transform this troublesome service into the long-desired corrections agency.

The document's key proposal was the replacement of existing non-custodial sentences with a single 'integrated' community sentence. This was not a new idea. The 1988 Green Paper considered and rejected it on the grounds that:

it might encourage the courts to impose too severe a penalty and make them more reluctant to use supervision a second time for an offender who had failed to complete an earlier order satisfactorily.   (3.33)

Instead, an additional order was suggested – the supervision and restriction order – whose details were virtually identical to those being proposed in the 1996 document. One of the main arguments against such an order at that time was its lack of *feasibility* (Carlen 1989). The assumption that offenders are prepared to do almost anything – however restrictive or degrading – in order to avoid going to prison has been shown to be quite erroneous (see Chapter 2). Probation officers have always known that there are limits on the demands that can be made on offenders and have constantly cautioned against 'setting offenders up to fail'. The cynical reintroduction of such ideas smacked of 'setting up' the probation service to fail.

But the impact of such a sentence on the *offender* was not the prime concern of the consultation document. Like the Green Paper before it, its main concern was to curry favour with the public in general and sentencers in particular. It reiterated the Green Paper's concern that sentencing should focus on restriction of liberty, reparation and prevention of reoffending. The reintegration of the offender into the community (or 'rehabilitation'), reinstated as a sentencing principle in the 1990 White Paper, was dropped once again.

As in the Green Paper, the consultation document fuelled and reinforced a public perception of non-custodial sentences which it had itself helped to construct. Compare these two excerpts:

> Not every sentencer or member of the public has full confidence in the present orders which leave offenders in the community.   (Home Office 1988:2)

> Community sentences . . . have failed to command the confidence of the public . . . probation supervision is still widely regarded as a soft option.
>   (Home Office 1995c:11)

But there has always been little evidence to support the view that sentencers want to be more involved in the detailed content of supervision programmes. Developments in pre-sentence report-writing which set out more explicitly than before what the probation service can offer have undoubtedly been welcomed. And the least contentious aspect of the consultation document was probably the proposal for the provision of feedback reports to courts on offenders' progress. Nevertheless, it seemed quite unrealistic to expect sentencers to draw up individualised packages of supervision for every defendant and the danger was that an informal 'tariff' would develop which may be every bit as inconsistent and court-specific as previous practice.

The document's one genuinely new proposal was the removal of the requirement for consent before the imposition of a community sentence. It could be argued that this was entirely consistent with the nature of the proposed 'community sentence'. Since the impact of the sentence on the offender is no longer a matter of concern to the court, there is no reason to perpetuate the myth of contract. It is also true, as the document argued, that what matters is not formal consent at the point of sentence 'but the offender's willingness to comply throughout the sentence' (11.4). Where the logic of this argument breaks down is in the assumption that the removal of formal consent will make no difference to the offender's co-operation. One cannot imagine anyone arguing that witnesses should not take an oath (or affirm) when they give evidence because what matters is not the oath but their 'willingness' to tell the truth! Many aspects of our criminal justice system are dependent on the significance of public declarations – it is part of our basic belief that 'justice should be seen to be done'. We know that the giving of consent to a probation order is no more than a residual ritual but it may have meaning for some offenders and it is, in any case, a useful negotiating tool for probation officers at the pre-sentence report stage. Its removal, by contrast, would be highly significant, for it demonstrates not only that the offender's consent does not matter but, yet again, that the probation officer's consent (to the wishes of the court) does not matter either.

The introduction of the generic term 'community sentence' by the Criminal Justice Act 1991 provided a helpful clarification of the role of non-custodial penalties in the sentencing framework, but it is difficult to see how 'the transparency of community sentencing' (5.2) could be increased by blurring the distinctions between existing disposals. On the contrary, an obvious criticism of the 'integrated' community sentence was that no one except the sentencing court and the supervising probation officer (and, it was hoped, the offender) would know exactly what it entails in any individual case. As far as the public is concerned, an integrated community sentence could mean anything – or nothing. The price of reducing public confusion about the differences between probation orders, community service orders, curfew orders and so on could be the reduction of all non-custodial penalties to their lowest perceived common denominator – the soft option.

Yet another truck on the punishment train

By August 1996, yet another truck had been coupled to the punishment train in the form of a White Paper entitled *Protecting the Public: the Government's Strategy on Crime in England and Wales* (Cmnd. 3190, Home Office 1996a). The Paper was not dissimilar in style and format to the 1990 White Paper which preceded the 1991 Criminal Justice Act. It set out the state of the art of criminal justice policy in the 1990s before making its four main proposals:

1 Abolition of automatic early release and its replacement by earned remission;
2 Automatic life sentences for second-time serious violent or sexual offences – 'two strikes and you're out', in popular parlance;
3 Mandatory seven-year prison sentence for third-time drug trafficking offences; and
4 Mandatory three-year prison sentence for third-time burglary offences.

The result of these proposals, it was admitted, would be to increase the prison population by nearly 11,000 by the year 2011, a statement which prompted (the then) Lord Chief Justice Taylor to describe the Paper as 'a bonanza for prison architects' (cited in Baird 1996). Unlike the 1990 White Paper, which admitted that prison 'can be an expensive way of making bad people worse' and that 'nobody now regards imprisonment as an effective means of reform' (Home Office 1990a:6), the 1996 Paper stated that 'the government firmly believes that prison works' (Home Office 1996a:4). Prison, it was now being argued, prevents crime by taking offenders out of circulation, it protects the public from dangerous criminals, its threat acts as a deterrent and it '*can* be used to rehabilitate offenders' (my emphasis). Perhaps most tellingly in relation to this book, we were told that 'criminals sent to prison are no more likely to reoffend than those given community sentences'. It may be for this reason that the chapter on community sentencing is notably thin and vague, apparently bowing to criticisms of the 1995 Green Paper and settling instead for supporting 'local demonstration projects' (Home Office 1996a:39). The White Paper gave the distinct impression that the government had finally given up on community punishment.

Conclusion

The 1991 Criminal Justice Act was the most significant piece of criminal justice legislation of the last quarter of the century. At the time, there was much criticism of it, but, in retrospect, there was probably more thought and consultation involved over a period of several years than one might have expected from a Conservative government that had been in power for over a decade. That it failed so spectacularly and so quickly was not the result of any long-term political conspiracy. Rather it resulted from a particular constellation of events occurring before the 'teething problems' of the Act had been resolved. In the prevailing political and economic climate of 'short-termism' (Hutton 1995) it was perhaps inevitable that kneejerk reactions would gain more credence than measured analysis.

Note

1   I am grateful to Gibson *et al.* (1994) for pointing out this phrase in David Garland's *Punishment and Modern Society* (1990:285).

CHAPTER 4

Constructing the punishing community

Introduction

The term 'community' is one of the most promiscuous words in contemporary political usage. It is attached to concepts hitherto regarded as falling within the spheres of either the private or the public. It is prefixed to innumerable 'feel good' words, such as care, centre, home, school, health, provision, transport, crime prevention, service and, of course, punishment. In so doing, it beguiles and seduces 'because it readily evokes images of neighbourliness, mutual aid, and a positive sense of "belonging" ' (Smith 1995:93). At the same time, critics would argue, it blurs the boundaries of responsibility (which is part of its appeal) and consequently (to continue the metaphor) it cheapens and degrades the original concept.

The aim of this chapter is to explore some of the connotations which the term 'community' has within criminal justice discourse. It will be argued that, while the term may appeal to a warm, nostalgic sense of 'belonging' among the self-proclaimed law-abiding, its promise of inclusivity can be interpreted in contradictory ways when applied to those who break the law and are criminalised. Far from demonstrating that it is resourceful, tolerant and healing, the community is then rejecting, excluding and intolerantly punitive. What, then, constitutes the 'community' in which offenders are to be punished?

Communitarianism, community and the individual

The term 'community' is rarely defined. It is a nebulous concept, which may be used to describe neighbourhood groups or whole nations, people with a community of interest (as in 'the gay community' or 'the deaf community') or people sharing a geographical identity and so on. Willmott's three-fold distinction between territorial communities based on geography, interest communities based on non-geographical common characteristics and attachment communities based on relationships with people or places is frequently cited (Willmott 1987).

However it is used, it implies at least two things. First, it *as*sumes an element of homogeneity based on common social characteristics, histories, traditions or beliefs. Second, it *pre*sumes that this homogeneity will manifest itself in a sense of mutual responsibility – a willingness to 'look after' or 'deal with' the needs of the members of the community. As Stanley Cohen says,

The iconography is that of a small rural village in pre-industrial society in contrast to the abstract, bureaucratic, impersonal city of the contemporary technological state.

(Cohen 1985:118)

There is nothing new about these assumptions and presumptions but their proliferation in political discourse has been a feature of the last two decades of the century and, in particular, a feature of the ideology of the New Right. Initially, this may appear to be a contradiction in terms since we tend to associate the New Right with neo-liberal individualism, self-sufficiency and non-interference by the state. However, by appropriating the concept of community, the New Right has emphasised less its collective responsibility *for* its members and more the responsibility of members *to* the community (Fatic 1995; Ireland 1995). In particular, it has stressed the 'rights' of the community to require certain standards of behaviour from its members and, ultimately, to exclude members in the interests of the whole community. This notion of community has little to do with the values of socialism and is now as much a part of New Labour thinking as of conservatism – the former emphasising the importance of 'new responsibilities to match new rights' (Ireland 1995:190).

The appeal of communitarianism lies in its ability to traverse the party political spectrum. By placing the community at the centre of our analysis and our value system, instead of either the individual or the state, we establish a social and political entity which is local enough to be both sensitive to our needs and controlling of our behaviour. The extremes of rampant individualism and dangerous socialism are thus rejected in favour of a theory which blends social construction (the individual is shaped by the social environment) and the localised emergence (rather than state imposition) of collective values such as reciprocity, solidarity and 'club membership' (Frazer and Lacey 1993). The fruits of community membership should be 'public goods' – a term which covers all provisions, facilities and practices from which members cannot be excluded. These may range from physically constructed facilities to public services and from utilities to routine, taken for granted freedoms and practices. What has become clear in recent years, however, is that few of these 'public goods' can any longer be taken-for-granted. Even fresh air is available increasingly only to those with the ability to live in certain areas and to avoid others. Less tangible public goods, such as 'justice', become problematic as people feel themselves increasingly obliged to 'contract into' provision for their own physical and emotional security. In such situations, it becomes debatable whether 'justice' can be described as a genuinely collective value or rather an aggregative value, the exact nature of which will depend on the cumulative interests of the individual club members (with their right to exclude those with different interests or those not subscribing to the club line).

Nor, as Frazer and Lacey (1993) demonstrate, does communitarian discourse in any way guarantee equality of access to the community's resources or 'club goods'. Communitarianism claims that moral and political values are generated and maintained by the community itself and are changed only through internal discussion, argument and conflict. The insularity of communities and the absence of 'debate across traditions and on the basis of values external to prevailing cultures' (Frazer and Lacey 1993:144) may result in the maintenance of sexist, racist or other discriminatory values and practices. There is nothing in the appeal to community which offers any fundamental criticism of oppressive traditional sexual divisions of labour or social practices of racial intolerance and exclusion. Club membership is not equally available to all, despite the powerful rhetoric to the contrary.

When we talk, then, about crime control being a matter for the community, or a community responsibility, it is by no means clear which particular brand of communitarian values are being expressed (Fatic 1995). On the one hand, we may be arguing that crime and criminals are a product of the community, that the causes of crime can be found in the material and social inadequacies of the community, that criminals are produced when individuals are denied their rightful share of the community's wealth and welfare. On the other hand, we may view the community as the upholder of positive values and moral virtues, as an environment of trust which is betrayed by the actions of criminals. Either way, the relationship between the criminal and the 'law-abiding' community is problematic, since the decision has to be made whether the criminal can or should be excluded from the community or reintegrated within it.

All of this is predicated on the questionable prior existence of an entity which is fundamentally cohesive, virtuous and, at least potentially, resourceful: the vision of an ideal community. Yet, as Frazer and Lacey argue succinctly, there is 'rhetorically powerful slippage between sociological and normative conceptions of community' (1993:154). The reality is that many of the communities most deeply affected by crime are fractured along hostile divisions of age, race and gender (Campbell 1993), exacerbated by endemic poverty and a chronic absence of resources other than those generated through the commitment of local interest groups (usually dependent on the skills and enthusiasm of particular individuals). For such people, an appeal to 'the community' is perceived only as an abandonment by official state agencies and a licence for certain groups of people (predominantly young men) to intimidate and destroy the neighbourhood (though for a discussion of the complexities of the relationship between intimidation and trust in communities, see Evans, Fraser and Walklate 1996). Although in many areas of mainland Britain, the meting out of this particular brand of informal or community justice is disorganised and haphazard, the phrase 'punishment in the community' has come to mean something very distinctive and chilling in the context of Northern Ireland, as McCorry and Morrissey (1989) make clear. Their account of a community project designed to protect juvenile offenders from both the formal systems of criminal justice *and* the punishment beatings and shootings of paramilitary organisations (supposedly supported by sections of communities who had lost faith in the ability of the formal systems to 'do anything' about 'ordinary' crime) provides a graphic illustration of the dilemmas facing those trying to help communities find genuine alternatives to unacceptably punitive existing options.

The connection between crime, community and the economy has perhaps been argued most accessibly in recent years by an economist rather than a criminologist. Will Hutton's damning indictment of what he perceives to be a society based on the worship of short-term profits and the dominance of shareholder interests blames our obsession with market processes for the creation of 'more and more poorly socialized children, teenagers and young adults' (1995:225). Unlike Charles Murray (1990), Hutton identifies the structural preconditions, rather than the personal inadequacies, which exclude many young people from educational and employment opportunities and condemn them to impoverished life chances and incomes. The result is a perfectly predictable breakdown of the informal control mechanisms which prevent most of us from committing the more visible and most publicly condemned acts of lawbreaking:

With the collapse of local communities there is less stigma attached to criminality, the informal sanctions and expressions of disapproval which offenders fear are no longer there; and they have little reason to empathize with their victims. There are fewer inbuilt deterrents and greater incentives to criminal behaviour.   (Hutton 1995:225)

Community policing and crime prevention

One attempt at restoring a 'sense' of community has been the emergence of community policing in the 1980s, following the Scarman Report on the 1981 riots. The Report highlighted the importance of active community consent for the actions of the police and warned of the dangers of jeopardising that consent. Community policing was also associated with John Alderson (1979), the former Chief Constable of Devon and Cornwall (Newburn 1995). Its aim was to restore the image of the police officer as the servant of the community, as a citizen with special powers and skills, maintaining order through consensus and dealing with emergencies of any kind. 'Solving crime' may form only a small part of the police officer's work and the use of force is only a last resort. Most of the time, 'good' policing is 'the craft of handling trouble without resort to coercion, usually by skilful verbal tactics' (Reiner 1994:721).

As Bennett (1994) points out, very few people object to the idea of community policing. 'It is almost like saying that you do not want the world to be a better place' (Bennett 1994:6). But what exactly is meant by community policing, what it is meant to achieve and how it can be evaluated, is elusive. It may be a useful shorthand for a desired ethos in policing 'which emphasises notions of service, the sensitive use of discretion, conciliation, consultation and negotiation' as opposed to an approach which is criticised as 'having lost touch with what the public wants, threatening civil liberties, invasive, oppressive, alienating and ineffective' (Weatheritt 1987:7). Alternatively, it may describe specific initiatives and practices: multi-agency liaison, work in schools, summer-holiday projects, local consultative groups and so on. Either way, the symbol of community policing is the bobby on the beat; its antithesis is the patrol car. Community policing, in theory at least, is about initiative and prevention rather than reaction and apprehension.

But the theory as well as the practice is flawed because community policing assumes that the interests and wishes of particular communities are compatible with the rule of law. Leaving aside for the moment the problems of defining 'community', there is a fundamental conflict between notions of decentralised policing and the universal framework of the law. What might be the implications if policing priorities were always determined by the wishes of local communities, or those self-styled 'community leaders' who purport to speak for them? As Smith points out:

At the extreme, law enforcement and order maintenance that is a response to the demands of local communities is equivalent to the rule of the lynch mob. The whole purpose of the law, it may be said, is to help us escape from the arbitrary judgements of our neighbours.   (Smith 1987:64)

Alderson's vision of a community policing itself following the example set by police leadership appears naïve when we begin to appreciate the narrowness of the borderline between community involvement in policing and vigilantism (Davies, Croall and Tyrer 1995). As Shapland and Vagg demonstrate, 'social order is continuously being constructed and negotiated' (1988:178) and we have constantly to ask the questions 'what community?', 'whose order?' and 'to whom are those who claim to be maintaining order accountable?' Unless these questions are asked and answered, the idea of community policing can become 'dangerously anti-democratic' (Loader 1996) because the false assumption is made that those who shout loudest and longest at police-community consultative committees are actually representative of the community as a whole. It is not the place of this book to engage in the debate about the future of policing, but Ian Loader's proposal for discursive policing, which encourages public dialogue about policies and practices while protecting the rights and values of the least powerful groups in society (for example, young people), is eloquently and convincingly articulated (Loader 1996).

Closely associated with community policing is community crime prevention, which Hope defines as 'actions intended to change the social conditions that are believed to sustain crime in residential communities' (Hope 1995:21). Again, what exactly is included in these 'actions' depends entirely on the standpoint of those who perceive actions to be necessary. Hope argues that the paradigm of community crime prevention has shifted from traditional (optimistic) concerns with community organisation, tenant involvement and resource mobilisation, through residential defence, prompted by the fear of crime and characterised by surveillance of various kinds (or 'watching') and finally to a paradigm of preserving order in disintegrating communities. The latter is characterised, on the one hand, by a belief that increasing the general control of disorderly public behaviour (or 'incivility') will contribute to crime reduction and, on the other hand, by a recognition that high crime rates may be at least in part due to the repeat victimisation of particularly vulnerable individuals. In this latter case, crime reduction may be brought about more successfully by targeting such individuals for attention. Crimes that are particularly susceptible to repeat victimisation are house burglary and domestic violence (Forrester, Chatterton and Pease 1988; Lloyd, Farrell and Pease 1994).

Involving the community in crime prevention has been a central concern of the Conservative government throughout the 1980s and 1990s. The symbols of such involvement have been closed circuit television (CCTV) and Neighbourhood Watch schemes. Despite the civil liberties objections, CCTV has been very widely accepted by the public (Groombridge 1995), though the problems of displacement (that criminals will simply go elsewhere) are beginning to be recognised. While CCTV is predominantly confined to high streets and shopping malls there may be few objections, but its extension to residential and semi-residential areas may meet more resistance. 'Freeborn Englishmen' do not readily subject themselves to invasions of their privacy and Garland's 'paranoid culture' (1995:3) lurks not far beneath the surface. It is one of the central arguments of this book that public opinion requires clear boundaries to be observed between conditions of freedom and conditions of custody, between public and private spheres.

Such ambivalence accounts, in part at least, for the limited success of Neighbourhood Watch schemes. A more significant factor, however, may be that of differential participation. Put crudely, those who need it least are the most likely to participate. Anti-crime groups are most likely to consist of the kind of people who participate in any kind of voluntary activity – the more affluent, better educated, longer-term residents with children and their own homes. Those on low incomes, living in rented accommodation in high turnover, deteriorating areas are least likely to participate (Hope 1995). For schemes to succeed, it seems, there need to be high levels of mutual trust and low levels of mutual suspicion within a community – yet precisely the reverse situation pertains in most high-crime areas.

Community and the victim of crime

Concern for victims of crime has increased in recent years, following accusations that the criminal justice system pays too much attention to the needs of offenders. In the past, there has been a tendency for victims to feel, at best, neglected and, at worst, blamed for their plight. Some victims complain that they are never informed about the progress of the offender through the courts or the outcome of the prosecution. Others have felt under pressure to co-operate with reparation or mediation schemes, whereby they meet with the offender in a situation that sometimes seems to be more for the benefit of the offender than the victim. Yet others experience traumatic ordeals when they are required to give evidence in court (Smith 1989).

Rape victims, in particular, may have to face the ordeal of being asked inappropriate questions about their sexual history (Smith 1989; Lees 1997). A victim may also find herself being directly cross-examined by her alleged perpetrator, sometimes for several days, if he chooses to represent himself legally in court. This latter situation has prompted calls for changes in the rights of defendants to represent themselves in this way.

The White Paper *Crime, Justice and Protecting the Public*, which preceded the Criminal Justice Act 1991, begins 'Too many people in England and Wales are hit by crime. Being a victim of crime and being frightened by crime stunts many lives' (Home Office 1990a:1).

The British Crime Surveys indicate that patterns of victimisation differ according to the offence and according to age, gender and lifestyle (Home Office 1995d). Most burglary victims live on poor council estates or in inner-city rented accommodation. Afro-Caribbean adults and single parents are particularly vulnerable, partly because of their residential and social circumstances. Young men are the most likely to be victims of violence or robbery, especially if they go out frequently, drink heavily and engage in 'boisterous' group activity. Women are more likely to be victims of theft, sexual assault and domestic violence. Serious assaults are far more likely to be committed by someone known to the victim than by a stranger. Probation officers make the point that offenders are often victims too. Many men and women in prison have been physically or sexually abused as children, or have themselves been victims of theft and burglary.

The government provides limited funding to Victim Support schemes, which offer emotional support and practical advice to victims of crime referred by the police. The first Victim Support scheme was launched in 1974 and by 1994 there were 376 such schemes with about 12,000 volunteers supporting over a million victims of crime a year (Home Office 1996a). Funding has increased from £5,000 in 1979 to nearly £11 million in 1995.

A further innovation in providing a better deal for victims is the Crown Court Witness Service which, following a pilot scheme in 1990, established a presence in 77 Crown Courts by 1996, offering advice, information and support to victims who have to appear in court (Home Office 1996a).

Courts attempt to take account of the needs of victims by making offenders pay compensation. In 1994, 90,000 offenders were ordered to pay compensation (averaging £183) in Magistrates' Courts and 6,600 offenders were ordered to pay compensation (averaging £2,087) in Crown Courts (Home Office 1995d). Applications to and awards from the Criminal Injuries Compensation Board (CICB) (available to victims of crimes of violence) quadrupled from 1979 to 1995 but only half of all applications are processed within a year. There are also a number of rules (for example, if the victim has a criminal record or in some way contributed to the incident) which enable the CICB to refuse or reduce compensation. From April 1996 the scheme was put on a statutory footing with a supposedly simplified tariff of payments, though critics claimed that this reduced payments to victims.

The increasing emphasis in official rhetoric on the needs of victims climaxed with the publication of the *Victim's Charter* in 1990, which ostensibly set out the standards of service which victims should expect from criminal justice agencies, but also made a clear statement about the future priority of victims in criminal justice discourse. Indeed, its significance did not lie primarily with its attempt to provide a code of practice, most of which was not supported by any legislation. The *Victim's Charter* is a document that lends itself to a number of 'readings' – not just as a policy document, but also as a political and ideological document (Mawby and Walklate 1994). In line with its development of the concept of social citizenship and the obligations of the individual to the community, the crime victim is constructed as a consumer of localised criminal justice services. The victim is a stakeholder in the process with rights as well as needs.

Of particular significance to the argument of this book is the emphasis on the accountability to victims of the criminal justice agency traditionally more concerned with offenders: namely, the probation service. The *Victim's Charter* began the process, requiring probation officers to take account of victims' views on the release of life-sentence prisoners. The setting up of a victims' helpline in 1994 to allow victims to ring prisons and express their fears about prisoners being released on home leave put additional pressure on probation staff both in assessing prisoner risk and in supervising home leave. The revised National Standards, produced in 1995, required probation officers to take account of victim impact when preparing pre-sentence reports. Finally, probation services have been encouraged to enter 'partnerships' with Victim Support schemes at a local level (Kosh and Williams 1995; Williams 1996c).

But the victim to whom all this refers is not every victim. This victim is constructed as structurally neutral (Mawby and Walklate 1994), without age, gender or class – the 'legitimate victim'. In order to be a legitimate victim, one is assumed to be a particular kind of person: an innocent child (who is abused), a helpless old person (who is mugged), a virgin (who is raped), a law-abiding pillar of the community (who is burgled). In other words, an image is created of a victim who is randomly selected and in no way contributes to their own victimisation. As soon as we move away from that pure and irrational image, we begin to rationalise why some people are victims and we begin to consider how they might have contributed to their fate. So the relationship or interaction between offender and victim starts to be constructed as significant and an object of examination and theorising. Judgements begin to be made about deserving and undeserving victims. Those deemed by the community to be undeserving may fare little better than offenders when it comes to seeking support and access to local resources.

Community and prisons

Perhaps the most controversial use of the word 'community' has been its coupling with 'prison' – a flagrant contradiction in terms, some might argue. The idea of the prison itself as a community is deeply embedded in a sociological literature which has, quite unjustifiably, become somewhat unfashionable (Worrall 1996b) but which it is not the purpose of this book to re-examine. Instead, a concept which has been a more recent addition to penal discourse – the community prison – will be explored, together with the reasons for its failure to materialise.

The Woolf Report into the prison disturbances of 1990 (Woolf and Tumim 1991) was wholly compatible with the Hurd vision of criminal justice. It was not a radical report (Sim 1994), but it sought to balance the demands of security and control in prisons with those of justice for prisoners, arguing that the disturbances of the previous year could only be properly understood if account were taken of the sense of injustice which many prisoners felt about their treatment. Among other concerns, one theme emerged which led Woolf to recommend a system of community prisons. Woolf's argument was that it was in the interests of both the prisoners' rehabilitation and the smooth running of the prison for prisoners to be accommodated as near to their homes and communities as possible. This could be achieved in one of three different ways. First, prisons should play a part in the community, involving outside organisations and individuals in work by or with prisoners – the concept of the 'permeable wall' (Penal Affairs Consortium 1994). Second, existing local prisons, which tend to be located in main population centres, could accommodate most prisoners for the whole of their sentences by providing differential regimes – the concept of the 'comprehensive prison' (Penal Affairs Consortium 1994). Third, clusters of prisons in a geographical area could be grouped together so that their differential facilities could enable prisoners to progress between them without having to move many miles away.

The idea was fraught with practical difficulties from the outset. How would smaller groups such as women and young offenders fit in? Could you include certain groups with 'special needs' such as lifers, vulnerable prisoners, high security risk prisoners? Nevertheless, for a short time, it caught the imagination of both the prison service and campaigning groups alike. NACRO, for example, produced a detailed report, both of the ways in which prisons could improve their links with local communities and of the ways in which new and existing prisons could be transformed into 'community prisons' (NACRO 1994).

But all this was based on the assumption that the 'community' wanted better links with 'its' local prison. As Roberts (1994) points out, however:

> The isolation of prisons from the community is a two-way process; and there are many people who would wish to increase the isolation and stigmatization of prisoners.
> (Roberts 1994:229–30)

Prisons are, after all, an expression of the community's desire to punish and exclude.

Apart from civilian employees (such as instructors, teachers and probation officers) and volunteers (such as prison visitors, the Samaritans and the WRVS), the involvement of the local community in the running of prisons is formalised in the role of Boards of Visitors. The role of prison Boards of Visitors is an important one in a democratic society (Worrall 1994a,1994b). Unpaid members of the public (appointed by the Home Secretary under the provisions of the Prison Act 1952) have unrestricted access to all parts of a prison at any time without giving notice. They can talk to any prisoner out of hearing of staff and must satisfy themselves 'as to the state of the prison premises, the administration of the prison and the treatment of prisoners' (Prison Rules 94(1)).

Until April 1992, Boards also adjudicated those prison disciplinary charges which were considered too serious to be dealt with by the governor. The loss of these powers, in response to the recommendations of the Woolf Report on prison disturbances, marked the culmination of a debate about role incompatibility which started with the Jellicoe Report in 1975 and was given its most comprehensive examination in the Prior Report into the prison disciplinary system in 1985.

The government argued that the central watchdog role of Boards had been hampered by its work on adjudications. First, it was argued that prisoners had little confidence in the inspection role of Boards, since they were perceived to be closely aligned with the establishment through their adjudicatory function. Second, adjudication proceedings were becoming increasingly legalised and subject to judicial review. In this climate Boards were said to be demonstrating their lack of competence to undertake adjudications. Increasing numbers of awards were overturned on judicial review and an experiment to introduce legally trained clerks to assist the procedures was said to have proved ineffective.

Credibility in the eyes of prisoners was not greatly enhanced by the loss of adjudications, according to research by Martin and Godfrey (1994). Part of the problem is that members of Boards, like magistrates, represent only certain sections of the local community. Research on the social characteristics of Board members (Worrall 1994a, 1994b) found very few respondents under 40 years of age and, for both sexes, the most common age category was 50–60. Most were employed in professional or managerial jobs. The second largest group of men described themselves as 'retired' and the second largest group of women as 'housewives' or 'voluntary workers'. Only five of the 100 respondents described their ethnic origins as anything other than 'white'. Despite recent efforts by Boards to recruit more widely through local publicity, more than 90 members had been recruited either through other involvement in criminal justice (e.g. as magistrates, solicitors, court clerks, social workers) or through other voluntary work which had brought them into social contact with existing Board members or prison governor grades.

In 1995 a further review of the role of Boards took place and an attempt was made to rename them (to resolve the long-standing confusion with prison visitors). Most Boards wanted the word 'Independent' to appear in their new title, underlining their detachment not just from local prison administration but also from government penal policy, of which they had become increasingly critical. The Home Secretary refused to countenance this and, since his own preference of 'Advisory Committee' was rejected by Boards, the name has remained. The point of this little anecdote is to demonstrate the subtle political shift in the role. No longer are Boards the representatives of the community who have direct access to the Home Secretary. Now they are directly accountable to him. The truth is that most Boards found themselves more in sympathy with the efforts of prison governors to provide constructive regimes in a hostile penal climate than they did with a Home Secretary who had no interest in 'positive custody'.

The concept of 'community prisons', along with much else in the Woolf Report, has been effectively abandoned. The Woodcock Report on the near escapes at Whitemoor, the Learmont Report on the breakout from Parkhurst, disturbances at Wymott, mandatory drugs testing, clampdowns on home leave, incentive schemes, according to King (1995), have served only to arouse fears

that the new emphasis on security, with its attendant changes in staff-prisoner relations, will simply store up control problems for the future ... Prison governors in future will obsessively but understandably watch their backs.

(King 1995:66)

The community and managerialism

The prison service, along with the police and the probation service, has become increasingly influenced by managerialist thinking. The key feature of managerialism in criminal justice is its emphasis on a systemic approach, which is more concerned with the bureaucratic-administrative relationship between various aspects of crime-handling than with the relationship (whether retributive or utilitarian) between the individual criminal and the state (and, by implication, the law-abiding citizens represented by the state).

Bottoms (1995:25) identifies four characteristics of the systemic approach: an emphasis on inter-agency co-operation; the creation of overall strategic planning (with separate but co-ordinated mission statements); key performance indicators to measure economy, efficiency and effectiveness; and, finally, active monitoring of aggregate information. Nothing, however, could be further from the concept of 'community' and herein Bottoms identifies a serious tension. The holistic nature of a community-based approach contrasts and conflicts with the 'componentiality and abstraction' of the managerialist approach (Bottoms 1995:39). An example of such tension is provided by Broad's study (1991) of a community probation team in Brixton in the mid-1980s.

'Can the probation service do both statutory work and community work?' asks a chief probation officer on a visit in 1985 to a beleaguered community probation team, set up in Inner London as a direct response to the Brixton disturbances of 1981 and the Scarman Report. He receives the answer he wants to hear: 'Yes, we've proved it's possible'. But the answer is disingenuous, for the team believes it has lost credibility as a result of lack of resources and lack of commitment by a management concerned only with centralised objectives and consensual politics, neither of which it perceives to be compatible with the decentralisation and adversarial approach essential for robust and effective involvement in a deprived inner-city community.

Broad's case study is based on empirical work carried out in the mid-1980s and charts, in compelling detail, the development of an official discourse which seeks to create a continuity between the concepts of 'punishment' and 'community'. It exposes the contradictions between a rhetoric that promotes 'patch-based', inter-agency co-operation and the reality of isolated, ill-directed probation officers, constrained by policies driven by the need to account for individual 'cases' and individualised problems.

Broad identifies three ways in which the term 'community' could justifiably be linked to the work of the probation service. First, **community probation work** continues in the service's tradition of focusing on individual offenders but seeks to enhance service delivery through greater use of community resources. Second, **crime prevention work** focuses on co-operation with other local organisations to reduce the levels of crime in the locality. Finally, **community work** would involve the service in locality development, social planning and social action for the benefit of all people living in the community, the assumption being that an improved environment and an enhanced sense of wellbeing will ultimately serve to reduce criminal activity.

From the outset, the commitment of the probation service to its experiment in Brixton seemed suspect. An early discussion paper concluded that 'what was not required was any radical departure from the central task of the probation service' (Broad 1991:60). That central task, according to Broad, is located within social control and social welfare models of community development. The former emphasises the need to police pathological deviant behaviour by the assertion of formal authority; the latter recognises the existence of individuals in need who can be helped – or helped towards self-help. Neither model takes serious account of social conditions, structural disadvantage or racial discrimination.

Broad's thesis, or 'prickly conclusion', is that unless the probation service breaks out of its consensual straitjacket and its need to

mirror wider control imperatives then progressive, effective and empowering probation community developments concerned with furthering social justice ideals, and restricting the worst excesses of crime will remain localised, discretionary and small-scale activities.   (Broad 1991:193)

Conclusion: the punishing community

The discourse of Punishment in the Community presupposes a mythical community which, to use Faulkner's analysis, is 'inclusive' (1996). Such a sense of community characterises a society which is open and compassionate and has confidence in its own future. It seeks to 'put things right' rather than punish, recognising the capacity of individuals to change and the obligation of the community to support and protect the vulnerable and disadvantaged. Carlen has used the phrase 'state-obligated rehabilitation' to describe the process (1989). By contrast, the reality of community is 'exclusive'. The criminal is seen as the enemy (as, for example, the hyena in the 1992 government advertising campaign against autocrime). We are engaged in a 'war' against crime, where there are two clear sides: the respectable law-abiding citizen and the feckless criminal outsider. *This* sense of community reflects an insecure society, suspicious of, and hostile towards, anything and anyone who is different. Community means segregation, prejudice and the desire for revenge.

The 'exclusive' community is the result of faith in the efficacy of the worst excesses of capitalism – unregulated competition and the survival of the fittest. Hagan (1994) parodies the language of capitalism by talking about *capital disinvestment:* the lack of will to invest in programmes that build up *social* and *cultural* capital.

In addition to *physical capital* (the tools, machinery, equipment, buildings and so on that are necessary for wealth production), and *human capital* (the skills and knowledge which are normally developed through education and training), Hagan argues that we stockpile *social capital*. This refers to the capabilities which are developed through social relationships, primarily through the family but also through other social attachments and commitments. Social capital is that stock of social skills and capacities which enable us to live and work together peacefully and creatively. *Cultural capital* refers to the ways we adapt to our heritage and our environment – whatever it is that we 'value' in our culture or cultures, over and above the imperatives of survival and wealth creation. Cultural capital may refer to our willingness to engage in higher education or the arts or conservation – and so on.

In order to maintain these forms of capital there must be *investment* by society. It is only through this investment that we will become *embedded* in the legitimate social and economic networks of our society. The notion of *embeddedness* means that we take for granted both the existence of certain structures and our own obligation to abide by the norms and values generated by those structures. At a personal level, it simply does not occur to us to behave in any other way. Hagan argues that we are experiencing instead *capital disinvestment*, by which he means the deliberate enhancement of inequality through policies of residential segregation (coupled with growth in private security), non-investment in poorer communities and collusion with racial discrimination. Such policies are destructive of social and cultural capital and lead to a dangerous process of *recapitalisation*. Recapitalisation refers to a reorganisation of available, diminished resources and the supplementing of these with illicit new resources in order to achieve goals. The most significant example Hagan gives of new illicit resources is that of drugs. The development of alternative structures and economic networks based on the economy of illicit drugs results in a new and oppositional kind of embeddedness, that of *criminal embeddedness*. The punishing community, far from encouraging reintegration and conformity, may instead be creating a 'parallel universe', reinforcing for some an embeddedness which takes for granted that the only way to behave is criminally.

PART TWO

THE CHANGING ROLE OF THE PROBATION SERVICE

CHAPTER 5

From 'advise, assist and befriend' to 'confront, control and monitor'

The role of the probation service in the criminal justice process represents at least two theoretical dilemmas: the extent to which criminal courts are obliged to follow the advice of non-legal professionals and the extent to which a balance can be maintained between care for an offender and control of an offender. It has been said that the probation service represents a mechanism whereby courts can institutionalise their ambivalence (Millard 1982). When requesting reports and when placing offenders on probation, they are admitting that they are unsure whether an offender should be punished or should receive help.

This chapter will focus on the history and traditions of the probation service and the impact of policy and legislative changes during the last quarter of the century. It will also engage with the debate about the training of probation officers which, it will be argued, has done more than any piece of criminal justice legislation to deprofessionalise the occupation. The removal of training from higher education and Home Office calls for more ex-servicemen and 'mature' people with 'authority' and 'common sense' to be recruited in place of liberal do-gooders has significant implications for the whole identity of the probation service. What sort of people will we have as the community punishers of the future and are these the people we want to be doing the job?

What the probation service does

The probation service is the major organisation in England and Wales for dealing with offenders in conditions of freedom. (In Scotland, the probation service ceased to exist as a separate organisation when it was incorporated into the new Social Services Departments in 1968; Northern Ireland has its own Probation Board.) Probation officers supervise adult offenders placed on probation by the courts and some young offenders under 18 years who are made subject to either probation or supervision orders (although Social Services Departments also supervise some juvenile offenders). Probation service staff also supervise offenders placed on community service orders and staff-approved probation and bail hostels. They provide what is called a 'throughcare' service for offenders sent to prison, which includes staffing a probation office in each prison and supervising prisoners on early release or parole. Probation officers prepare pre-sentence reports on offenders to help courts to arrive at the best sentencing decision)(for further discussion see Chapter 6).

A probation order is a community sentence which requires an offender to be supervised by a probation officer for a minimum of six months and a maximum of three years. Under the Criminal Justice Act 1991 a probation order may be made on any offender over the age of 16, although the juvenile equivalent, a supervision order, remains an available option for 16- and 17-year-olds. A probation order can only be imposed with the consent of the offender, although, as we saw in Chapter 3, there have been attempts by the Home Secretary to abolish this requirement.

The probation order has a long history dating back to the Probation of Offenders Act 1907. It was originally intended to be an *alternative to a sentence* and remained so, technically, until the Criminal Justice Act 1991. Its traditional purpose was to offer advice, assistance and friendship to offenders, in the belief that they could thus be reformed or rehabilitated. More emphasis is now placed on restricting offenders' liberty, although under the Criminal Justice Act 1991, the objectives of a probation order still include the rehabilitation of the offender, as well as protecting the public and preventing reoffending. The conduct of probation orders is governed by National Standards, issued first in 1992 and revised in 1995. Their significance is discussed later in this chapter.

Offenders sign a contract that, while on probation, they will keep in touch with their designated probation officer through regular office appointments and visits at home. They must also notify their probation officer of any change of address or employment. If they fail to meet these requirements they may be subject to breach proceedings, which means that they are taken back to court and resentenced. Probation officers have been very reluctant in the past to institute breach proceedings because most view it as undermining their rehabilitative role (Lawson 1978), though a few 'breach enthusiasts' adhere to the belief that breach is just, beneficial to the offender and important for the credibility of the probation service (Drakeford 1993). For many years the proportion of orders terminating for failure to comply with requirements (where no new offence was committed) ran at 2 per cent annually. Since 1989, however, this proportion has crept up and was 4 per cent in 1994 (Home Office 1996b).

Since 1948 it has been possible for courts to add conditions to a basic order requiring an offender to live at an approved residence or to undergo psychiatric treatment. More recently, courts have been able to require an offender to attend programmes of activities at a probation centre for up to 60 days (or longer for sex offenders).

Advocates of the traditional probation order extol its flexibility as a sentencing option. They argue that it can be used for relatively minor and serious offences and can be tailored to the particular needs of an offender. However, it has been hard for the probation order to shake off its image in the eyes of the courts as a 'soft option', suitable only for less serious offences. After the introduction of community service in the 1970s, the use of the probation order declined dramatically. In response, the probation service emphasised its value as an *alternative to custody* for serious offences. After the Criminal Justice Act 1982, the use of the probation order for men increased from about 29,000 in 1984 to 40,000 in 1994. By contrast, orders for women declined in the same period from about 11,000 to under 9,000 (Home Office 1996b). This may be explained by the success of probation officers in persuading the courts that most offences committed by women are insufficiently serious to warrant supervision, but the steadily increasing numbers of women sent to prison suggests that a more contradictory logic of 'bifurcation' is in play.

Since the 1991 Criminal Justice Act, probation orders can now be combined with community service orders in the form of combination orders. The rationale for this is to provide courts with an additional community sentence which offers help to the offender while also exacting reparation. Such orders have proved popular with the courts, their numbers having increased from 1,400 in 1992 to nearly 15,000 in 1995 (Home Office 1996c).

Following one amalgamation, there are now 54 probation areas in England and Wales (mostly coterminous with counties), employing around 7,800 probation officers, 1,900 probation services' officers (formerly known as ancillary workers), 4,800 clerical and administrative staff, and 900 non-probation officer staff in approved probation and bail hostels (Home Office 1996b). In the ten years from 1984 to 1994, the proportion of female probation officers rose from 39 per cent to 52 per cent. In 1994, approximately 7.5 per cent of probation staff were recorded as belonging to an ethnic minority group. This is slightly higher than the proportion in the general population but while the proportion of Afro-Caribbean staff was about twice that in the general population, the proportion of South Asian staff was about half of the comparable group in the general population.

The Home Secretary is responsible to parliament for the work of the probation service, whose interests are dealt with by the Home Office Criminal Department. The Home Office provides 80 per cent of the probation service's funding, the other 20 per cent coming from local authorities. In each probation area there is a Probation Committee or Board, consisting of magistrates, judges, local authority representatives and independent people. They have responsibility for the management of the probation service, including the appointment of probation officers.

Each probation area has a chief probation officer with overall responsibility for the direction and delivery of service in that area. Responsible to the chief probation officer are deputy and assistant chief probation officers who usually have responsibility for particular aspects of service (for example, training, prisons) and/or geographical regions in the area. Senior probation officers are in charge of teams of probation officers covering a geographical 'patch' or a specialism such as courts, community service or probation centre. Most teams include a probation services' officer who is not professionally qualified, as well as clerical and administrative staff. Attached to many teams are probation service voluntary associates who are ordinary members of the public, assisting probation officers in such tasks as befriending and transporting clients.✶

✎In the past probation areas have enjoyed relative autonomy to develop their own policies and practice but the service has become increasingly centralised, particularly since the publication by the Home Office in 1984 of the *Statement of National Objectives and Priorities*. Since that time, central government has sought to standardise practice across England and Wales and probation officers now work within the framework provided by National Standards, which set out the expectations and requirements of all aspects of supervision.

There is considerable disagreement about the extent to which the probation service can be regarded as a social-work organisation. Until the mid-1990s, in order to be appointed as a probation officer it was necessary to have a professional social-work qualification (the Certificate of Qualification in Social Work, the Certificate in Social Service or the Diploma in Social Work) but the Home Office Green Paper *Supervision and Punishment in the Community* (1990b) argued that more emphasis should be placed on the service's role as a criminal justice agency and, for the first time, hinted at the possibility of significant changes in training and recruitment. Before pursuing that particular debate, a brief account of the history of the probation service will illustrate how the service found itself facing such a threat to its professional status.

The history of the probation service

The probation service has its roots in the work of the nineteenth-century police court missionaries, first employed by the Church of England Temperance Society in 1876 to 'reclaim' offenders charged with drunkenness or drink-related offences. The Probation of Offenders Act 1907 gave Magistrates' Courts the right to appoint probation officers, whose job it was to *advise*, *assist* and *befriend* offenders placed under their supervision.

The Criminal Justice Act 1925 made it obligatory for every court to appoint a probation officer and during the first half of the twentieth century the work of the service expanded to include work with juveniles and families, as well as adult offenders. Part of that work included dealing with matrimonial problems and it was through this aspect of the work that the role of the Divorce Court Welfare Officer developed. By the mid-1960s the service had also taken responsibility for the welfare of prisoners, both inside prison and on release. The distinctive professional skill which probation officers developed was that of the Social Inquiry (or Enquiry) Report. This was a social-work assessment of an offender in his or her social environment, with a specific purpose of assisting courts to make sentencing decisions.

The 1991 Criminal Justice Act changed the name and, some would say, the purpose of reports. The content of pre-sentence reports is laid down in National Standards but normally includes information about the offence, especially its seriousness and the offender's attitudes and circumstances. It concludes by proposing possible appropriate sentences. The main difference between a social inquiry report and a pre-sentence report is that the former traditionally placed greater emphasis on the personal and social circumstances of the offender, while the latter is primarily concerned with the seriousness of the offence and the offender's attitude towards it, though this is a rather crude distinction, as will be seen in Chapter 6.

✳ Although there had always been a degree of tension in the role of the probation officer between *caring* for offenders and *controlling* their criminal behaviour, these two aspects of the work were viewed as part and parcel of both the psychoanalytic casework and the paternalistic 'common sense' advice which combined to characterise the typical probation officer of the early and mid-twentieth century. By the end of the 1960s the Probation Service had grown from the status of a localised mission to that of a nationwide, secular, social-work service to the courts. Its expansion had been unselfconscious and the concepts of care and control had not been incompatible. The service's three-fold function apparently caused no crises of conscience: ₅

1 Advisers to courts – both criminal and civil;
2 Supervisors of offenders in the community; and
3 Supporters of prisoners and supervisors of ex-prisoners.

From the 1970s onwards a number of developments had paradoxical consequences for the service and resulted in a loss of identity, or, to use Harris's (1980) term, 'dissonance'. Harris argued that probation officers were experiencing three kinds of dissonance in their work:

1 Moral dissonance, resulting from conflicting ideologies about the purpose of probation;
2 Technical dissonance, resulting from discouraging empirical evidence about the effectiveness of probation in reducing criminal behaviour; and
3 Operational dissonance, resulting from tension inherent in managing the 'care and control' aspects of the daily probation task.

Three ideological conflicts permeated the probation service in the 1970s. These can be summarised as, first, the conflict between *genericism* and *specialism*; second, the conflict between work with *low-risk* and *high-risk* offenders; and, third, the conflict between *ideological trade unionism* and *pragmatic trade unionism*.

The Seebohm Report of 1969 heralded the age of genericism in social work and by 1971 the new Social Services Department had been established. Prior to this, social workers had been divided into a number of occupational groups – such as childcare officers, mental welfare officers, hospital almoners – each with their own identity, tradition and training. Some families had several different welfare workers offering unco-ordinated and sometimes stigmatising services and at great cost. The ideology of Seebohm was that the new social workers should be able to offer a comprehensive generic service to families in need, rather than a series of specialised interventions. To complement this radical change in service delivery, a new national training body – the Central Council for Education and Training in Social Work (CCETSW) – was created and, along with it, a new generic qualification – the Certificate of Qualification in Social Work (CQSW) – located in universities, at a mixture of undergraduate, postgraduate and non-graduate level.

The equivalent development in Scotland was introduced a little earlier by the Kilbrandon Report in 1968 and the probation service in Scotland agreed to be incorporated into the new Social Work Departments. In England and Wales, however, the probation service fiercely defended its independent identity and remained separate. It did, nevertheless, join in with the new training proposals. Prior to the establishment of CCETSW, probation officers had been trained on a short specialist course run by the Home Office (though it is interesting to note that when the course started in 1930, there was an assumption that recruits would already have a university diploma in social science – see Le Mesurier 1935:66) and this option continued to be available until the late 1970s. However, it tended to be used primarily for mature, second-career recruits who could not afford, or were not sufficiently academically inclined towards, the two-year CQSW courses. Increasingly, recruits to both Social Services Departments and the probation service were young, academically able and politically radical. The Home Office, which had supported the retention of a separate probation service, became increasingly alarmed at its inability to control the content and tone of the training of probation officers.

On the same day as the new Social Services Departments came into being, the 1969 Children and Young Person Act was implemented – or, at least, as much of it as was ever implemented. This landmark piece of legislation will be discussed in more detail in Chapter 10 but the important point to note here is that it aimed to remove juvenile offenders from the stigmatising effects of courts and probation service supervision. Instead it invested the power to care for juvenile offenders in the new Social Services Departments. The logic of this lay in the belief that juvenile delinquency is a product of unsatisfactory upbringing and socialisation within the family and that the welfare of juveniles should be of greater concern than their punishment.

But the new breed of generic social workers was viewed with distrust by the police and magistrates when it came to their ability – and their willingness – to control the behaviour of troublesome young people. Magistrates frequently compared social workers unfavourably with probation officers. Brown (1990) identifies three reasons why magistrates were uncomfortable about social workers. First, they had a fear of unfamiliar colleagues. Magistrates lacked the opportunity to meet social workers, who were less frequently in court than probation officers. They did not understand the social work 'culture' and did not see social workers as being in the same business. Second, they perceived social workers as lacking expertise in the 'rules of the game' in court (see Carlen 1976). They feared that social workers lacked tactical sense and might rock the boat or do something embarrassing. Third, social workers were perceived to be too theoretical, jargon-bound and idealistic – they were viewed as driven by left-wing ideology, lacking 'common-sense', making 'unrealistic' recommendations in their reports.

Parker, Sumner and Jarvis found similar views among the magistrates they interviewed:

The best social workers were lost to early retirement. The new breed of whizz kids go to Keele [*sic*] for two years, have their brains removed, get a plastic card with their picture on it and think they're a social worker.

(Parker, Sumner and Jarvis 1989:95)

The upshot of this was that magistrates were reluctant to commit juvenile offenders into the care of social workers. The original intention of the 1969 Act was that very few offenders under 14 years of age would be brought to court at all and that offenders aged 14–17 would be supervised by social workers. Very quickly it became apparent that courts wanted probation officers to continue to supervise older juveniles and, because of the confusion about responsibilities between the two agencies, the safest option for magistrates seemed to be to send increasing numbers of juveniles to detention centres or to the Crown Court for borstal sentencing (which was outside their powers), so that they would eventually be released on 'after-care' to the probation service. This was totally contrary to the spirit of the 1969 Act and was certain to bring about its failure. True, the numbers cautioned rose dramatically, but the numbers placed on supervision or in care declined and the numbers sent to detention centre or borstal escalated from 2,500 in 1968 to 7,500 by 1978 (Pease and Bottomley 1986). It was a classic case of 'net-widening' and 'up-tariffing'. The welfare approach so widely condemned as a feature of the 1970s did not, in reality, ever happen.

The consequence of 'hiving off' juveniles to Social Services was that the probation service was enabled to work more with 'high-risk' offenders. (The fact that many juveniles were artificially reconstructed as being 'high risk' by the process just outlined is another of the ironies of that decade.) The 1972 Criminal Justice Act introduced community service (see Chapter 7) and day-training centres (see Chapter 8), planting the seed of 'alternatives to custody' rhetoric and the greater surveillance of offenders. But the most controversial development was to be found in the recommendations of the Younger Report in 1974. One aim of the Younger Report was to rationalise custodial provision for young adult offenders, by replacing prison, borstal and detention centres with a single 'custody and control' order. But its more controversial proposals were based on the belief that to reduce the numbers of young people in custody one had to 'strengthen' community supervision (a familiar net-widening fallacy). A new 'supervision and control' order was proposed which did not require the offender's consent and also gave probation officers the power to request the police to detain a 'client' already on supervision for up to 72 hours in order to forestall the commission of an offence. The recommendations were greeted with alarm by most probation officers (for a discussion of the arguments, see the Special Younger Report Issue of *Probation Journal*, Vol. 21, No. 4, December 1974) and were never implemented but a re-reading of the Report 20 years on will demonstrate that many of the contemporary debates about 'care versus control' are by no means new.

The third continuing conflict concerned the development of the probation service's sense of its own occupational identity and its relationship with other workers – and not just those in the criminal justice system. During the 1970s, the National Association of Probation Officers developed from a 'cosy' professional association to a trade union representing an increasingly well-trained profession. Politically increasingly left-wing and concerned to promote the ideology of radical social work within the criminal justice system and beyond, it campaigned on ideological grounds to withdraw from staffing Prison Welfare Departments, to refuse to write Social Inquiry Reports in 'not guilty' pleas and for the right to demonstrate in solidarity with workers not directly concerned with criminal justice (participation in the Grunwick dispute leading to the suspension from NAPO of its London branch). Bitter wranglings in NAPO over the issue of *ultra vires* led to new objectives to broaden legitimate interests of NAPO in social as well as criminal justice. But this was set against the constraints of the general economic climate of the 1970s and the decline in the use of traditional probation orders. In order to avoid cuts, the probation service identified with the 'law and order' lobby of the new Thatcherite government and sold itself directly as a service which could help reduce numbers in prison by offering effective alternatives.

The rise of managerialism

We saw in Chapter 2 how, under the umbrella of the Financial Management Initiative which emphasised economy, efficiency and effectiveness, the Home Office, which had previously adopted a *laissez-faire* attitude to probation areas, decided to reassert its control.

Following the 1984 *Statement of National Objectives and Priorities*, and their own subsequent local responses, the probation service began to engage the services of financial management consultants. In this it was reflecting the increased use of management science in the public sector, but the most visible effect on probation officers was their perceived loss of professional autonomy and a greater emphasis on accountability through the devising of team and area objectives, action plans and so on.

In 1989 the Audit Commission reviewed the service and concluded that it was not giving value for money. A similar, but lower profile exercise went on in relation to probation training, which was funded through sponsorship by the Home Office. As a result of the Coleman Review, the Home Office decided to be far more directive about the content of probation-training programmes in an attempt to socialise students better into the ideological and bureaucratic demands of the service and rid them of left-wing indoctrination by ivory tower academics. It paid scant regard to the fact that CCETSW itself had already embarked on a major overhaul of social work training which was to go some way towards answering the Home Office's concerns. The new Diploma in Social Work required every course to be accountable to a local consortium, or partnership, of social work agencies, to ensure that students were being trained appropriately to meet the demands of an ever-changing social work scene. Local probation services became the driving forces behind a number of these partnerships and, as a result, expressed increased confidence in social work training – a message which did not please the Home Office!

Alongside the White Paper *Crime, Justice and Protecting the Public* (Home Office 1990a) which sets out the government's philosophy for criminal justice, based on the principles of 'just deserts' came two further Green Papers: one on the organisation of the probation service and the other on partnership with voluntary agencies.

Supervision and Punishment in the Community (Home Office 1990b) was designed to rationalise the structure and organisation of the service and to limit the autonomy of individual probation areas. It proposed greater central control and possible amalgamations of smaller services. It also reinforced the role of the service as a criminal justice agency (rather than a social work agency) which should relate primarily to other criminal justice agencies – the police, prisons and, above all, the courts. It stated that the probation service must be so organised as to ensure:

- Responsiveness to criminal justice policy;
- A clear framework of accountability;
- Effective management;
- Value for money;
- Confidence of sentencers; and
- Effective links with other organisations in the community.

It raised again the question of probation officers' training and suggested

that social work training might not be the most appropriate route to qualification. It made a number of alternative proposals, including a free-standing probation qualification, and asked for views.)
⊣ Similarly, the (pale) Green Paper, *Partnership in Dealing with Offenders in the Community* (1990c), was intended to make clear to the service that it did not have a monopoly on punishment in the community and that the privatisation of community sentences might well follow prison privatisation (Matthews 1990). When the probation service had refused to have anything to do with electronic monitoring during the 1989 pilot schemes, the government saw a golden opportunity to begin thinking about contracting out the supervision and surveillance of offenders.

To complete the chronology of this particular round of multi-coloured papers, a blue 'Decision Document' entitled *Organising Supervision and Punishment in the Community* was published in April 1991 which dealt with structural organisational changes aimed at rationalising the service, limiting its financial resources and making it more accountable to other criminal justice agencies, especially the courts.

The loss of professional autonomy

But we might argue that all these developments, while affecting the managers and policy-makers in the service, would still leave the grass-roots probation officer with her professional autonomy in respect of her individual cases. Even the 1991 Criminal Justice Act did not impinge directly on that.

But *National* Standards did. From 1989 to 1992, the Home Office compiled a series of National Standards directing practice in relation to all aspects of probation service supervision: report-writing, supervision and probation orders, community service orders, new combination orders, the management of hostels, and supervision during and after imprisonment. They cover not just broad policy guidelines, but detailed instructions about the administration of orders. They cover frequency of contact, record-keeping, rules about enforcement and the taking of breach action, and the content of supervision sessions.

There were some good professional justifications for National Standards, and few disputed the need to standardise some very variable and inconsistent practices across the country and between individual officers. Professional autonomy had undoubtedly been used in the past as an excuse for poor practice. Also, if anti-discrimination was to be taken seriously, then there had to be an attempt to ensure minimum standards of service delivery.

However, National Standards must also be seen as the government's attempt to make individual probation officers more accountable to management and management more accountable to the government. They fit nicely with the rhetoric of the Citizen's Charter and the rights of –

well, whose rights? – to be reassured that criminals are being adequately supervised. It is not without significance that the revised *National Standards* of 1995 downplay their value to offenders and other service users. While the 1992 version stated that offenders 'should have access to a fair and effective complaints system if they are dissatisfied with the service they receive' (Home Office 1992b:3), the later version stresses that they 'should be informed of what is expected of them and the action which will be taken if they fail to comply with the requirements of the standards' (Home Office 1995e:2).

The overriding point about the introduction of National Standards was that they limited the discretion of the individual probation officer and focused on the management of supervision rather than on its content. And it followed that the need for probation officers to undertake two years' training as social workers, when all the procedures they will ever need to follow were now laid out in a glossy ring-bound booklet, must be open to question.

The stage was set for the final onslaught on probation training. In 1994 Vivienne Dews of the Home Office reported on a training scrutiny and recommended the removal of sponsorship from most Diploma in Social Work programmes, despite widespread satisfaction among local probation services (Ward and Spencer 1994; Williams 1994). She favoured the retention of a few centres of excellence but expected most recruits to the service to be trained on the job, perhaps through the competence-based framework of National Vocational Qualifications (NVQ). Both routes would lead to a new 'Diploma in Probation Work'.

In February 1995, the Home Secretary took the decision to repeal the legal requirement for all new probation officers to hold the Diploma in Social Work, thus ending the control of higher education over probation training. The decision was justified on two grounds: first, that since Social Service social workers are not required by law to have a social work qualification, why on earth should probation officers be required to do so? and, second, that existing training selection discriminated against mature students, particularly men who had relevant experience and skills (for example, in the armed forces). The first argument was, logically, the stronger but politically weak, since most people agree that more social workers, rather than fewer probation officers, should be professionally trained. The second argument was disingenuous in the extreme, since the probation service has always recruited a proportion of older second-career men. But it has insisted on retraining them. Even more invidious was the appeal to broader recruitment on implied equal opportunity grounds, which temporarily seduced some into thinking that there might be more opportunities for black people and women to join the service. This was emphatically not what Michael Howard had in mind – indeed, even the Dews Report had identified the high proportion of younger women joining the service as a 'problem'.

The rest, as they say, is history. There were many campaigning comings and goings but, by 1996, there were no Home Office sponsorships for Diploma in Social Work programmes and on-the-job training was developing fitfully. Probation services themselves largely gave up the battle because financial restraints were so severe that there were no jobs to recruit into anyway. On the contrary, services were 'downsizing' and looking for early retirements among existing staff.

Some might say that in this, as in other aspects of the job, the probation service precipitated its own downfall with its constant criticism, over the previous decade, of social work training. Particularly damning was research undertaken in the late 1980s by Davies and Wright (Hardiker and Willis 1989) which purported to show that probation students on social work courses considered themselves ill-equipped and inappropriately trained for their future employment. But reminding the service of this seems rather distasteful – like suggesting that a dear friend might have contributed to his own death by reckless behaviour.

Problem-solving to impression management

For a number of decades, probation officers saw themselves, rightly or wrongly, as professional social workers, working in the specialist setting of the criminal justice system. They believed they possessed a body of knowledge, had developed particular skills and had an ethical base to their work. As such, they had a right of discretion and control over their own work. That professional autonomy has been steadily eroded to the point where many probation officers see themselves as nothing more than criminal justice operatives, concerned only with the technological aspects of a bureaucratic job.

Shaw (1987) writes about the erosion of control which school teachers have over their work and he argues that the same analysis could be applied to social workers (and for a later comparison of the teaching and probation professions see Williams 1996a). Shaw's concern is that the loss of control and the acceleration of managerial and bureaucratic demands mean that workers are so preoccupied with the minutiae of their jobs that they either lose sight of, or are too exhausted to take interest in the wider social, economic and political influences that ultimately shape the nature of their work. If they manage to remain aware of them, then they are broadly integrated into the hegemonic establishment as a service class of junior partners.

Shaw argues that the mass professions like teaching and social work are unavoidably untidy, indeterminate and unpredictable because they are dealing with human beings in changing social circumstances. Attempts by the government to tidy up probation and make it more efficient and effective are linked with the desire to reduce opposition to government criminal justice policy and to locate the blame for its failure to reduce crime at the lowest level possible – namely, at the level of face-to-face contact with offenders.

It is not insignificant that the people who underwent the greatest amount of in-service training in relation to the 1991 Criminal Justice Act were probation officers. Magistrates, lawyers, police and prison personnel received far less training. Probation officers may feel that this was indicative of their importance on the criminal justice stage but a different interpretation might be that they were being set up as the people to blame when things started going wrong.

The probation service was therefore shifting from being what May calls a 'problem-solving' organisation to a 'performance' organisation:

The clients' problems are not then considered central, but impression management for the government and the Home Office is. (May 1991: 169)

Critique of the management ideal

There have been a small number of voices seeking to resist the hegemony of managerialism and the foreclosure of the management debate in the probation service (including Humphrey 1991; Humphrey and Pease 1992; May 1994; Beaumont 1995). Perhaps the most persistent has been that of McWilliams (1990, 1992). He argues that the management ideal masquerades as a set of 'value-neutral techniques with claims to the detachment of a science' (1990:60). It is, on the contrary, a system of thought which incorporates ideas about the nature of relationships – in the case of relationships with offenders, that they should be tough and confrontational – and on the ethics of actions – that they should be procedurally standardised, efficient, economical and capable of being monitored.

National Standards, he argues, are a mixed blessing for three reasons. First, they legislate only for minimum standards, discouraging innovation and diversity; second, they relocate discretion up a hierarchy away from the professional practitioner, stifling initiative; third, they shift attention away from the intrinsically individual nature of the rehabilitative and reformative processes.

The management ideal, he argues, makes the probation service vulnerable to change imposed from outside because it starts at the top with policy that is 'given'. The role of managers is merely to translate that policy into instrumental objectives and to ensure, through evaluation and monitoring, that organisational practice is commensurate with those objectives.

McWilliams proposes an alternative model of organisational arrangement which he calls an 'Administrative/ Professional Leadership Model'. This model is based on an appreciation of the nature and purpose of the probation service which is concerned more with its identity – what it is – than with what it does. This involves a leadership which embodies the values and professional practice of the service, leading by example, and an administrative framework which enables those who work within the organisation to express those values in their tasks and practices. Improvement in performance standards comes through feedback, dialogue, encouragement and critical analysis. Supervision is characterised by consultation and advice, rather than by its contemporary characteristics of line management. Officers would be held *substantively accountable* for their professional decisions and actions, rather than *formally accountable* for the procedures they follow. In short, he yearns for a return to a participative model of organisational accountability.

Perhaps unsurprisingly, McWilliams was perceived as an idealist by many in the probation service. Shepherd (1991), in his response to McWilliams, argues that his critique of management is simplistic, vague and unduly negative and that his alternative model is so nebulous that it is extremely difficult to imagine how it would work. He argues that what McWilliams is talking about is bad management, not management *per se*. On the contrary, he believes that good management benefits the probation service in the following ways:

- Recognising that staff are an organisation's most valuable asset and maximising their potential;
- Recognising that staff work best if they are clear about what is expected of them;
- Holding staff accountable;
- Ensuring staff have the resources to do the job;
- Encouraging creativity within the boundaries of policy; and
- Ensuring that decisions are made on the basis of the service's values and not individual whim.

Conclusion

The probation service has developed in little more than a century from being a localised, voluntary, evangelical outreach provision to being a profession whose work is integral to the criminal justice system. It is not unreasonable, however, to suggest that it may be a profession in decline. Having consciously adopted the 'high-risk' strategy of focusing on 'high-risk' offenders and having conceded the right of central government to dictate its priorities, it was bound to become vulnerable if the penal climate were to get any colder – as it has done. Once the need for probation officers became politically open to question, it was perhaps inevitable that the service would have to face the deprofessionalisation of its workforce.

The probation service has become very defensive about its management and it is now very difficult to challenge the received wisdom of its 'mission'. Ken Pease, a professor of criminology who has had a great deal of experience of working in association with the probation service, has said:

I have found Probation managers over the [past] decade to have been very sensitive to external criticism, far more so than the police service over the same period. Some conflict in organisations is healthy but . . . many of the conflicts surrounding probation management do not feel good.

(Pease 1992:x)

CHAPTER 6

Taking the 'social' out of inquiry reports

Introduction

This chapter will discuss the role of the probation officer in court – as an 'expert witness' – and his or her relationship with sentencers. The social inquiry or enquiry (there has never been any logical reason for the different spellings) report has been the traditional mechanism for the reconstruction of a criminal within professional discourse as a 'treatable' or 'manageable' offender. It has symbolised individualised sentencing based on the positivistic (or humanistic) belief that an understanding of the offender's personal and social background and circumstances may contribute towards helping him to stop offending. The 1991 Criminal Justice Act replaced the social inquiry report with the pre-sentence report and this represented much more than a change of nomenclature. It represented an uncoupling of the relationship between crime and 'the social', locating it firmly in the realm of 'the moral', the main focus being individual intentionality, remorse and capacity to respond to normalising instruction.

Nearly a quarter of a million reports are prepared every year – some three-fifths for Magistrates Courts and the remainder for Crown Courts. It usually takes probation officers three weeks to prepare reports, although they can be written more quickly if this is considered essential. Probation officers normally interview a defendant twice and one interview may be at the defendant's home in order to assess his circumstances. Relevant personal information is gathered and then verified as far as possible. The defendant's attitude to the offence is assessed and possible sentences are discussed. Some sentences, such as probation orders and community service orders, require the offender's consent so it is important that the offender understands what is involved. Probation officers have to try to ensure that they conduct the interviews and write the reports in a way which accords with anti-discriminatory practice. They have to take account of the fact that black people and women may experience discrimination in the criminal justice system. To this end, some probation officers ask colleagues to read their reports (a process known as 'gatekeeping') to help them identify any discriminatory language or comments (Raynor, Smith and Vanstone 1994).

Until the 1994 Criminal Justice and Public Order Act, courts were required to obtain reports before passing certain sentences, such as custodial sentences and certain community sentences. Since that time, they have had wider discretion to pass a custodial sentence without reports but they still often ask for reports in these and other cases (Charles, Whittaker and Ball 1997). There is an assumption that the defendant has already pleaded, or been found, guilty. In the Crown Court, reports sometimes have to be prepared before a trial for practical reasons and this presents a problem. It has been argued that it is unethical to write a report which advises on sentencing when the defendant has not yet been found guilty of the offence.

↳ Harris has said, 'Social inquiry reports are the main vehicle for routine interchange between the probation service and the courts' (1992:148). Their content, structure, style and philosophical underpinnings are symbolic of the whole relationship between social work (in the form of the probation service) and criminal justice. Their significance is much greater than the factual accuracy of the information they contain about an individual offender, although criticism of their role has often focused narrowly on that aspect. Their origins are clearly rooted in the rehabilitative individualised approach to sentencing which emphasises personal histories and circumstances and it has not been easy to adapt them to a 'just deserts' approach which focuses more on the offence than the offender. ǀ

The history and development of court reports

Providing personal and social information on an offender to a court has always been a key feature of the job of the probation officer. Le Mesurier (1935) talked of 'investigation' and described its purpose as being 'to strengthen the hands of the court in dealing with the individual offender' (1935:89). She talked about the importance of magistrates understanding the offender's personality, his needs and potentialities. She set out guidelines to both the content of a report (under the two headings of 'environment' and 'personal history') and the process of information-gathering. The probation officer should 'avoid too much direct questioning' and 'over-insistence on points of detail'. In short:

> He must be a good listener, sympathetic but unbiased, neither critical nor condemnatory, but unemotional and quite 'unshockable'. (Le Mesurier 1935:95)

So, although from the outset reports were intended as sentencing aids, they were also much more than this. They were intended to be diagnostic tools, similar in many ways to the social histories taken by a doctor or psychiatrist. Probation officers saw themselves as professionals making diagnostic assessments about the causes of offending and the treatment appropriate for each individual offender. Although Le Mesurier talks about the interests of the offender and the interests of the community, she does so in the same breath and makes no reference to any conflict between the two. What is the right treatment for the individual offender is also assumed to be in the best interests of the community.

This optimistic, positivistic, scientific approach reached its zenith with the Streatfeild Report of 1961. Its purpose was to examine the role of probation reports in the context of what was perceived to be a changing sentencing climate – a gradual shift from backward-looking concerns about culpability to concerns about how to influence future behaviour (Bottoms and Stelman 1988). The key to this influence was seen to be the provision of information that was comprehensive, reliable and relevant to sentencing. The probation report (renamed the social enquiry report by the Morison Report of 1962) had to provide three kinds of information:

(a) Information about the social and domestic background of the offender which is relevant to the court's assessment of his culpability;
(b) Information about the offender and his surroundings which is relevant to the court's consideration of how his criminal career might be checked; and
(c) An opinion as to the likely effect on the offender's criminal career of probation or some other specified form of sentence.

(Bottoms and Stelman 1988:23)

The assumptions underlying Streatfeild were that such information existed and that it was obtainable, communicable and utilisable. The belief was that sentencing was rational and scientific and that probation reports could both reflect and contribute to scientific research about explanations for crime and the efficacy of particular treatments for particular sorts of offenders. Reports were therefore professional documents of the assessment of culpability and risk.

Unfortunately, attacks on rehabilitation in the 1960s and 1970s, called into question the existence of any reliable knowledge about the effects of treatment on offenders. In addition, critics were increasingly pointing to a gap between rhetoric and practice. Research suggested that even basic information was gathered and presented in a haphazard and inconsistent manner (Perry 1979; Thorpe 1979) Academic courtroom observers commented on the strategies used by probation officers to maintain their credibility with magistrates while appearing, to the untrained eye, to be seeking lenient sentences for their clients (Carlen and Powell 1979). Radical socialist probation writers Walker and Beaumont (1981) wrote a searing indictment of social inquiry report practice, claiming that probation officers had neither the time nor the skills to make the kind of claims that were routinely made in reports. They identified a 'front region account' corresponding to the Streatfeild model, which was presented to magistrates and researchers and which contrasted with the 'back region account' of interviews conducted in competition with children, television, neighbours and animals:

It is not easy to concentrate with a demented budgie sitting on your head or a large Alsatian sniffing up your skirt.   (Walker and Beaumont 1981:16)

Probation officers were increasingly criticised for making personal moral judgements in the guise of professional assessments and of contributing to erratic and discriminatory sentencing. Harris concludes:

Empirical research into the quality, content, consistency and impartiality of SERs found them wanting and probably incomprehensible to their subjects, disappointingly few of whom possessed the social science degree which would have enabled them to have understood the more linguistically and conceptually complex of these documents. (Harris 1992:146)

He quotes Barbara Wootton who was on the Streatfeild Committee as saying in 1978:

I welcome social enquiry reports because they make me feel cosy, inasmuch as they transform a 'case' into a human being but, sadly, I am driven to the conclusion . . . they do little to make me in any sense a better sentencer.
(Harris 1992:146)

Bottoms and Stelman (1988) suggest that, in addition to Streatfeild's model, there are two other ways of looking at the significance of social inquiry reports. The first is within the penal analyses of Foucault (1977) and Garland (1985), based on notions of hierarchical observation and normalising judgements. The second (to be discussed later in this chapter) is the administrative, systems-management approach advocated by Tutt and Giller (1984) and containing the seeds of pre-sentence reports.

In *Discipline and Punish*, Foucault (1977) talks about the 'examination' which combines 'hierarchical observation and normalising judgements'. He talks of the 'normalizing gaze' which makes it possible to qualify, classify and punish by making individuals visible and then differentiating and judging them. The purpose of social inquiry is therefore to control or discipline offenders by placing them in pre-conceived categories which trigger particular responses – a sophisticated way of distinguishing between the deserving and undeserving. Much of the advice offered to social workers about conducting social inquiry was designed to enable the worker to 'catch out' the individual being investigated. Bottoms and Stelman cite Donzelot (1980) who, in turn, quotes a 1920s article on social inquiry. The article contains the same advice as that given by Le Mesurier but Donzelot interprets it very differently. The investigator was advised to find out everything on record about a person before visiting them, to talk to anyone respectable who might know them, to make surprise visits – first in the afternoon to catch mother alone and then in the evening to see if father gives the same story – to examine the home for evidence to support or refute the offender's story. But all this was to be done pleasantly, in order to encourage the person to talk as much as possible – and presumably to give themselves away!

This pessimistic approach to social inquiry fits the model of the disciplinary society constructed by Cohen (1983, 1985). What matters here is not so much the detailed accuracy of the content of a report but the image of the offender which is represented by the report. This analysis has been particularly relevant to reports written on women and black people where stereotypical representation has been seen to adversely affect sentencing practice.

Social inquiry reports, women and black people

In the early 1980s[1], the main concern among those practitioners who were prepared to cast a critical eye over their practice was that too many women were being placed on probation at too early a stage of their criminal careers. Although women offenders represented between 15 and 17 per cent of all known offenders, they accounted for about one-third of all probation orders. With increasing awareness of the dangers of net-widening (thanks largely to the insights of writers in the field of juvenile justice) an optimistic view emerged that reducing the numbers of women on probation would result in a reduction in the numbers of women being sent to prison. (This optimism proved quite unjustified, as will be discussed later.) The social inquiry report was identified as a key document in the social construction of female offenders as suitable candidates for supervision. Worrall (1981) and Eaton (1985, 1986) drew attention to the dangers of seeking to locate such women within the ideology of the nuclear family and of portraying (or failing to portray) them as good wives, mothers or daughters. By comparing reports on men and women, and the differential use of home visits by probation officers preparing reports, Eaton (1986) also highlighted the significance of differing gender-role expectations in reports. Such expectations go beyond a description of a conventional division of labour in the home to the belief that women have a responsibility for the emotional well-being of everyone in the domestic sphere. Even when they themselves are law-abiding, they are expected take some responsibility for – or at least shed light on – the offending behaviour of male partners. The reverse is rarely the case.

In a statistical comparison of court disposals of male and female defendants, Mair and Brockington (1988) concluded that women tend to be referred for social inquiry reports more readily than men (when offence and previous record are matched) and are more likely to be recommended for (and to receive) probation orders. Mair and Brockington observe that there is some evidence that referral for reports is in itself likely to move a defendant 'up-tariff' and that this should be a matter of concern for a service seeking to target reports on specific groups seen to be at risk of custody.

Deciding when a female offender is 'at risk' of custody, however, has been a vexed issue. Jackson and Smith (1987) found that many women are in prison for an accumulation of minor offences, having been considered unsuitable for community service as a result of domestic responsibilities. Similarly, Dunkley (1992) found a lack of consensus among probation officers about the appropriateness of referring women to day centres (now probation centres). Consciousness of sentencing discrimination may lead one officer to recommend Centre attendance to forestall a custodial sentence, while another officer may view such a recommendation as collusion with that same discrimination.

Representing women in social inquiry reports as 'programmable' – as motivated towards and able to benefit from the resources of the Probation Service – requires their construction within the discourses of domesticity, sexuality and pathology (Worrall 1990/1995). It is an exercise fraught with dilemmas:

> The trap for probation officers who might want to construct female lawbreakers within alternative discourses is that, in an area where such stereotypes dominate, they run the risk of seriously disadvantaging their client. Hence many officers justify their continued writing of gender-stereotyped reports on the grounds that they are working tactically in their clients' best interest. (Worrall 1990/1995:116)

Stephen (1993) confirms the view that female offenders are 'muted' (Worrall 1990/1995). Although their own accounts of their offending differ little from those given by men (and are predominantly based on external social factors), they are more likely to find their accounts disregarded by probation officers, who apparently still tend to prefer seeing women's crime as the result of 'underlying emotional problems'. Female offenders are still not being listened to.

Very little research exists which is specifically concerned with the portrayal of black women in social inquiry or pre-sentence reports. Denney (1992) suggests that probation officers tend to write assessments of white women offenders which are more detailed and sympathetic than those of black women. There is a tendency to assume that at the root of black women's offending lies a problem of identity resulting from not belonging to the dominant culture. While white women may be portrayed as neurotic and irrational, black women are portrayed as unpredictable and 'suffering from a peculiarly "feminine" form of "silliness" ' (Denney 1992: 109). Chiqwada (1989) argues that racism in social inquiry reports is more overt:

> Black women may be seen as over-protective, over-religious or over-punitive, and labelled as "bad" mothers. Expressions of emotion, whether anger or affection, may be misinterpreted. Similarly, value judgements concerning issues such as sexual or family relationships, work status, parental responsibility based on a Eurocentric view of society, are then used to justify prison sentences.
>
> (Chiqwada 1989: 104)

Although little has been written specifically on black women, there were a number of small-scale research projects in the 1980s concerned to identify any differences in reports written on white and black men that might account for the disproportionate numbers of black people given custodial sentences. The details of these, sometimes conflicting, studies have been well-documented (see, for example, Reiner 1989 and Denney 1992) and it is possible to extrapolate from them three broad conclusions, reflecting a lack of understanding and confidence on the part of white probation officers when faced with black (often young and usually male) offenders.

First, there was a tendency for probation officers to fall back on racial and cultural stereotypes, attributing offending to unconventional family structure and socialisation, or to cultural tensions and conflicts, especially among 'second generation immigrants'. Second, probation officers tended to include information which might appear routine and morally neutral, such as nationality and place of birth, but which might nevertheless serve to create an image of the offender as different – as Other – and as requiring special treatment by the court. Third, several studies found that probation officers were reluctant to make firm recommendations for non-custodial sentences for black people. This was not necessarily attributed to direct racism on the part of probation officers, but more to an inability to develop sufficient rapport with an offender to create the kind of relationship in which supervision might be seen as having any potential. Unfortunately, some of the anti-racism training given to probation officers during that time made the situation worse rather than better. White probation officers lost their professional confidence and came to believe that they did indeed have very little to offer young black offenders. Consequently, recommendations for probation became even fewer with the result that more black people were given prison sentences.

Since the 1991 Criminal Justice Act and, in particular, section 95 (see Chapter 2), probation officers have been provided with a 'Checklist for Anti-Discriminatory Pre-Sentence Reports' (Sanders and Senior 1994: 156–7). The checklist addresses five broad areas of discrimination – race, gender, sexual orientation, poverty/unemployment and disability – and takes the officer step by step through the process, content, proposals and outcomes of the report. It offers some sound practical advice such as allowing adequate time to discuss issues of discrimination, telling the offender what is going into the report in good time so that any errors can be corrected, creating a 'conducive' environment for interview and not being oppressive (shades of Le Mesurier?) It also, however, poses some unanswerable questions such as:

How can structural inequalities re housing, education, benefits etc. be included when relevant, without stereotyping?

Check out own value judgements/belief systems to see how they influence content.

Check that any community sentence proposed will not further contribute to discrimination.   (Sanders and Senior 1994:156–7)

If we could answer these questions, we should undoubtedly go a long way towards the elimination of discrimination!

Tutt and Giller and the Home Office

In response to criticism about the value of social inquiry reports, the

Home Office issued guidance during the 1980s which was aimed at making them more focused documents, concerned with very specific issues rather than claiming to be all-purpose generalised assessments of people and their lives. In doing this, they were influenced by work at Lancaster University which Norman Tutt and Henri Giller (1984) did in relation to juvenile justice and court reports. This work was based on three assumptions:

1 That behaviour is often situation-specific rather than being the product of enduring personality traits;
2 That reports can contribute to stigma and labelling and thus amplify deviance; and
3 That rehabilitation does not work.

Therefore, reports should be seen as limited exercises, intended solely to help decide what should happen to an offender as a consequence of committing a particular offence. They should be aimed at negotiating the least restrictive sanction commensurate with the seriousness of the offence. They are aids to administering or managing the criminal justice system in relation to an individual offender. They do not cover everything in the offender's life and they do not cover all the considerations which the court may take into account, for example, harm to the public, the prevalence of a particular offence, local reaction and so on.

Report writers were decreasingly being trusted as 'experts' and were increasingly being required to spell out both the process of their inquiries and the details of their recommendations. For example, they were required to state their sources at the beginning – where they got their information from and what steps they had taken to verify it. They were also required to spell out in the conclusion exactly what a probation order would involve and why it was seen to be suitable. In other words, probation officers could no longer get away with saying 'in my opinion'. They had to produce the evidence to support their arguments and be prepared to defend it in court. They could no longer hide behind their professionalism.

It has been argued (Worrall 1990/1995) that, in making sentencing recommendations, probation officers are faced with the dual dilemma of defining the appropriate 'moment of intervention' and defining the appropriate 'nature of intervention' in relation to any given potential client. That decision is made as a result of a professional assessment of the relationship between client need, agency resources and client motivation (that is, the extent to which the client's expressed desire to change is judged by the probation officer to be 'genuine' and the extent to which he is judged to have the capacity to benefit from the resources available). That assessment must then be translated into language which is acceptable to the court. The defendant must be presented in a form which is recognisable by solicitors, psychiatrists and, above all, sentencers.

Traditionally, probation officers have claimed authority for such reports on the grounds that they contain recommendations of 'expertly selected treatment based on scientific diagnosis' (Raynor 1985:153). By the mid-1980s, however, probation officers were more modest in their claims:⊁

> Any opinion expressed in the report about the appropriateness of some form of contractual sentencing ... should be offered to the court as a plausible alternative to the retributive tariff sentence ... The important issues are what the offender is prepared to do, whether and how far the social work agency is able to help him do it, and what assurances the court will require from both parties.
>
> (Raynor 1985:153)

Pre-sentence reports and predicting risk

The increased focus on the offence rather than the offender culminated in the change of name to that of pre-sentence reports. As we have seen in Chapter 2, the underlying philosophy of the Act was one of 'just deserts' or the imposition of a sentence which is commensurate with the seriousness of the offence. The assessment of offence seriousness became one of two new skills required of probation officers in writing court reports – the other was risk assessment. The two are connected but they do not amount to the same thing. Probation officers have always been concerned with assessing risk in the sense of preventing, reducing or deterring recidivism. They have been less concerned with assessing the seriousness of an offence, preferring to see that as a moral rather than professional task and, therefore, as the job of the court. They have always sought to 'second guess' the court's view of the seriousness of an offence and have taken that into account, but they have not seen it as something for which they themselves have a direct responsibility.

The requirement that probation officers should now contribute to (or, some might say, collude with) an assessment of the *seriousness* of an offence subtly removes one area of potential conflict within the court. Probation officers are required not just to take account of how they think an offence might be perceived by others (which is fair enough). They are now required to enter that moral debate directly and take responsibility for making a moral judgement, based not on any professional knowledge but on sheer common sense. In fact, the moral question was quickly reduced to an administrative one and Gilyeat (1993) soon provided a handy *Companion Guide to Offence Seriousness*, with scales and diagrams to help the report writer calculate the number of applicable mitigating and aggravating factors and thus locate the offence in the right classification: 'less serious' (recommend discharge), 'serious enough' (recommend community sentence) or 'so serious' (abandon hope).

The task of *risk* assessment has proved more complex and more elaborate mechanisms have been devised for the purpose. The first explicit use of the term in relation to social inquiry reports was by Curnock and Hardiker (1979) who, coming from a mainstream social work tradition, argued that social inquiry reports require the writer to balance the *risk* posed by the offender with his *needs* and with the *resources* available to him (that is, personal, social and professional resources). Bottoms and Stelman (1988) elaborated further on the concept of risk, arguing that the report writer should distinguish between the risk of reoffending and the risk of the damage caused by reoffending to the offender and his family and friends. They dismissed a third distinction – that of risk to potential victims – as being a matter for the court and not the report writer. They went on to outline two sets of hazards which together might constitute a risk assessment. *Predisposing hazards*, based on research, suggest that reoffending is most likely to occur among young men whose first conviction was at an early age, who have a large number of previous convictions with no recent break in the pattern, who have previous experience of institutions and who commit offences alone. By contrast, the least likely to reoffend are older women with late first convictions, few previous convictions with a long gap since the last conviction, who have no previous experience of institutions and who commit offences in company. The seriousness of the current offence appears to have no direct bearing on the likelihood of reoffending. *Situational hazards* refer to factors specific to the individual offender and the circumstances surrounding the commission of the offence. Are the circumstances which gave rise to the offence likely to recur? Does the offender have a particular personal or social characteristic which makes him vulnerable (for example, an uncontrollable temper, a drink problem, debt)?

The process described here might be termed 'soft' risk assessment, since it is based on the subjective professional opinion of the probation officer, using his or her knowledge and skills to 'paint a picture' of the offender in his environment. Such an approach became less and less acceptable both to the probation service and the courts.

One of the earliest attempts to assess risk more 'objectively' was the Cambridgeshire Risk of Custody (ROC) Scale devised by David Bale (1987). The ROC scale consisted of a form which sought to quantify all the factors which courts might be expected to take into account (such as offence gravity, criminal history, age, gender and so on) and which would then provide a percentage likelihood of an offender receiving a custodial sentence (the risk score). This would then guide the probation officer in making their recommendation. Unfortunately, it was never made clear whether the scale was intended to be predictive (that is, what the court *would* do) or normative (what the court *should* do). Nor was it clear whether its purpose was to enable the probation officer to 'second guess' the court more successfully or to influence the court away from its most likely disposal (Raynor, Smith and Vanstone 1994). In the end, most officers used this, and other versions of ROC scales as aids, which gave them an indication of the relative likelihoods of custody for different groups of offenders. Bale himself conceded that 'the best probation officers will always out-perform a fixed scale, even if I have demonstrated that the scale can out-perform the average officer' (1987:127).

It might be argued that risk of custody is not the same thing as the risk of reoffending, which in turn is different from the risk of harm. Probation officers' inability to separate these different issues has led to a great deal of 'fuzzy thinking' (Kemshall 1995, 1996; Webb 1996). In her research on risk assessment in pre-sentence reports, Kemshall found that officers were using a range of criteria that might well be challenged by a critical outsider as being little more than 'common sense'. Notions of risk were based on perceptions of 'unpredictable' behaviour, attitude to the offence, offender characteristics, motivation to change and so on. The only situation in which officers seemed willing to apply rigid procedures was in the case of sex offenders, but this, Kemshall suggests, was more to cover themselves than to protect potential victims. In most other cases, because the risk was diffuse, it was also more difficult to calculate and to grasp.

Kemshall concludes that there is no easy route to risk assessment and that 'fuzzy thinking' is not necessarily dangerous, 'for risk itself is fuzzy, changing constantly with differing probabilities and differing impacts for different people' (1996:7). Although the term 'fuzzy' is one which most academics would balk at, the idea that risk, in this context, cannot be quantified actuarially is not exactly novel and it is telling that the probation service needs to be reminded of that. The term 'risk' has been widely explored in recent years in criminological literature and it is unfortunate that the insights offered by such people as Katz (1988) and Beck (1992) have been ignored. Risk-taking is now a well-recognised motivation for criminal activity and unless that can be incorporated into probation officers' and sentencers' understandings, there is little hope of accurately calculating the risk of reoffending or the risk of harm. But discussion of 'risk-taking' is not acceptable in the discourse of pre-sentence reports – it is part of the 'social' which has been ejected from the exercise.

Conclusion

The content of reports is now heavily circumscribed by policy statements and National Standards and this, together with concerns about the potential dangers of discriminatory language, has meant that reports have become much more bland documents. That transformation of the 'case' into the human being is no longer obvious and one suspects that many reports could be produced by computer software. They have become part of the administration. The probation service has always rightly seen reports as the public face of probation – as a skilled strategic document (even long after the demise of rehabilitation) which encapsulated the ethos of the service. If recommendations have not been followed then the service has tended to blame its own lack of skills in communicating its message. But a message has a receiver as well as a sender and however sophisticated the sender may try to make the message, it will not be effective if it does not resonate with the receiver's own frame of reference – if the receiver is not prepared to listen. At the moment, the receiver –

the sentencer – is not being encouraged very strongly to listen to the message.

Note

Pages 82–83 have been reproduced by kind permission of Jessica Kingsley Publishers from G. McIvor (ed.) (1996) *Working with Offenders*, Research Highlights in Social Work 26.

CHAPTER 7

Demanding but not degrading? The appeal of community service

Industrialist: We attach a lot of importance to your research on this product, you know.
Researcher: What happens if the research shows that the product is a winner?
Ind: We'll go ahead and introduce it quickly.
Res: What if the research shows it's a loser?
Ind: We wouldn't want to hold back on a good product like that on the basis of one little piece of research.   (Pease 1983:78)

Introduction

From its introduction in 1973 the role of community service has been ambiguous yet increasingly popular. Its chameleon-like ability to adapt its aims and objectives to fit almost every traditional justification of punishment has made it as versatile as the fine – indeed, it has been described as a fine on time. But the incongruity of using unpaid supervised work schemes as a form of punishment at times of high unemployment in the community as a whole has never been seriously questioned. Community service raises fundamental questions about our perceptions of both 'community' and 'service'.

Community service, which requires offenders to undertake unpaid work, is a relatively recent penal innovation, although its predecessor, hard labour, has a very long history. Since the 1960s, various forms of community service have developed in many countries, notably in America, Australia, Canada and New Zealand. It is interesting, however, that some countries have resisted it on grounds of principle and practice. In Spain, for instance, it was feared that rising unemployment would undermine its credibility and in Sweden it was felt that not only would it not reduce imprisonment but that work should be viewed as a privilege, not a punishment (McIvor 1992). Community service has been most popular in England, Wales and Scotland where it has been used for a wide variety of offenders. By contrast, it has been underused in America, where it tends to be used for white-collar offenders, juveniles and minor offenders only (McIvor 1992; Tonry and Hamilton 1995).

The history of community service

Community service emerged in Britain as a result of increasing concern about the rising prison population in the 1960s coupled with attacks on rehabilitative treatment. It was one of the recommendations of the Wootton Advisory Council on the Penal System in 1970 and was described as the 'most imaginative and hopeful' of its recommendations. It was incorporated into legislation in the 1972 Criminal Justice Act and six experimental pilot schemes were set up in 1973, under the responsibility of the probation service.

A community service order requires adult offenders to perform between 40 and 240 hours of supervised unpaid work, to be completed within a year. Failure to complete the order satisfactorily can result in a return to court and a sentence of imprisonment. The 1982 Criminal Justice Act subsequently extended community service to 16-year-olds but reduced the maximum order to 120 hours. The 1991 Criminal Justice Act abolished that limit. It is only available for imprisonable offences, but from the outset there was confusion about whether it was a direct alternative to custody or whether it could be used as a sentence in its own right. This confusion meant that there was concern among some in the probation service that it would be used too early in a criminal career and thus accelerate an offender's route into prison. It was seen as a gap-filling measure which was in danger of being a net-widening sentence. Some probation officers initially refused to co-operate or to recommend the sentence.

Although Home Office researchers evaluated the experiments (Pease *et al.* 1975), their concerns were largely disregarded in the government drive to extend provision throughout England and Wales by 1975. Pease was later to comment scathingly that

> the realization that the community service research was not meant to inform the decision about whether community service orders should continue or should cease involved a reappraisal of what should be included in the research report.
>
> (Pease 1983:78)

Fundamental questions were jettisoned in favour of administrative ones. Because of this and the lack of consensus about the purpose of community service, inconsistent practices developed across probation areas. The main inconsistencies were in relation to:

- What kind of offender was suitable;
- What kind of work was suitable; and
- What standard of attendance and work was acceptable.

In 1977 *Probation Journal* devoted a complete issue to reviewing the first five years of community service. The editorial asked the questions 'What exactly is the purpose of a community service order? What has the probation service made of this new provision?' There followed several heart-searching articles, all of which, though cautiously optimistic about community service, were conscious of its contradictory underlying penal philosophy and its challenge to traditional perceptions of the probation officer's job. Pease and McWilliams (1977) identified four ways in which community service differed from traditional work:

1   The need to view the offender as a giver rather than a consumer of help;
2   The specificity of the contract between court and offender (and implications for breach);
3   The degree of contact between the probation service and the community; and
4   The way the service's performance is assessed by itself and by others.

The use of community service increased during the 1970s and levelled off in the 1980s at 7–8 per cent of sentences for indictable offences, compared with 10 per cent for probation orders and 14 per cent for immediate imprisonment. In absolute figures, there were 41,000 community service orders made in 1991, compared with 45,000 probation orders. From 1992 onwards, however, numbers of community service orders overtook those of probation orders, the former rising to 50,000 and the latter to 49,000 in 1994 (Home Office 1996b). However, while about 18 per cent of probation orders were made on women, only 5 per cent of community service orders were on women, comparing more closely with the proportion in prison.

The kind of work undertaken varies greatly but can be categorised in three ways:

- *Workshops:* manual work such as woodwork, metalwork or textiles, undertaken on probation premises, often to order for voluntary organisations and charities;
- *Supervised teams:* primarily gardening and painting and decorating for elderly people, or renovation work for churches and other voluntary organisations, supervised by sessional supervisors; and
- *Agency placements:* individual placements in nurseries, residential homes or any other voluntary organisations, supervised by that agency.

National Standards and community service

In 1989, in an attempt to standardise practice, the government issued **National Standards** for community service. The purpose of these statutory rules was to make the order appear to be harsh punishment, to control offenders' choices, to impose greater structure on working arrangements and to enforce discipline and required standards of work (Vass 1990). In particular, they addressed the kind of work being undertaken. National Standards require the probation service to provide a range of placements, including 'at least one option providing hard manual work and consideration should be given to choosing placements which enhance public confidence in community service' (Home Office 1995e). Although the 1992 version of National Standards suggested that placements should also be 'personally fulfilling' (Home Office 1992b:70) for the offender, the 1995 version exhorted probation services to 'ensure that the location and nature of any community service activity could not give the impression of providing a reward for offending' (Home Office 1995e:35). A new prohibition on placements abroad seems to be a response to media criticism of a highly imaginative and altruistic project devised by Surrey Probation Service to undertake work in Romania in 1990 (Whitfield 1993). A similarly subtle shift of emphasis can be seen in the stated aims and objectives of community service. Both versions include 'reparation to the community' as an aim, but a comparison of the remainder of the relevant sections is illuminating:

The main purpose of a CSO is to re-integrate the offender into the community through positive and demanding work, keeping to disciplined requirements.'

(Home Office 1992b:67)

The main purpose of a CSO is to *prevent further offending* by re-integrating the offender into the community through *punishment*, by means of positive and demanding *unpaid* work, keeping to disciplined requirements.

(Home Office 1995e:34, emphasis added)

Additionally, National Standards require clearer recording of hours worked and clearer procedures for breaching an offender in the event of failure to comply. Community service orders have always had a higher rate of breach procedures than have probation orders, rising from 11 per cent in 1985 to 18 per cent in 1991 (following the introduction of National Standards) and falling back to 15 per cent in 1994 (Home Office 1996b). Hine and Thomas (1995) suggest that this demonstrates an ethos in which breach proceedings are regarded as a 'first resort' rather than a 'last resort', with the expectation that courts will issue a warning and allow the order to continue, thus reinforcing its authority. Vass (1990), however, questions whether the increased structuring of community service may not be counter-productive in the long term since the success of community service depends on sophisticated negotiation between supervisor and offender, including a degree of tolerance of technical rule infraction. National Standards, he argues 'may well structure community service but they will not destructure the prison' (Vass 1990:131).

The main change introduced by the 1991 Criminal Justice Act was the **combination order** which allows courts to combine a probation order with a maximum of 100 hours of community service. Previously, the rationale behind the two sentences had been viewed as incompatible – an offender required *either* help and advice *or* to engage in reparation – and the two could not be used together at the same time. In practice, however, many offenders found themselves on both orders as a result of multiple court appearances, and the government sought to eliminate what it saw as an anomaly. In fact, it was introducing yet another net-widening disposal, destined to draw offenders nearer to custody (Moloney 1995). Combination orders quickly proved a popular disposal, their numbers rising from about 1,350 in 1992 to nearly 15,000 in 1995. Of these, about half include the maximum 100 hours of community service (Home Office 1996b, 1996c).

Penal philosophy and community service

The absence of a clear philosophy for community service has been both its strength and its weakness. Its weaknesses have already been outlined. Its strength is that it appeals to a wide variety of people, not least offenders themselves, for a wide variety of reasons. Duguid (1982) summarises its attraction thus:

- *It involves punishment.* Regular attendance at placements deprives the offender of free use of his leisure time.
- *It has a rehabilitative element.* The offender must spend time helping others and this may help restore a sense of dignity and self-esteem, as well as improving the community's perceptions of the offender.
- *It contains an indirect element of reparation.* The work benefits the community in general and/or specific, often disadvantaged, sections of the community.
- *Unlike prison, it allows the offender to retain a job and to support a family.* If unemployed, it may help the offender to develop a work habit and to overcome social isolation.
- *It saves public resources and is arguably cheaper than prison.*

(Duguid 1982 cited in McIvor 1992:9)

Research

One of the most recent research studies on community service is by McIvor (1992) whose research is based in Scotland. She undertook a comprehensive study over five years from 1986 to 1991, looking at the characteristics of offenders selected for community service, the nature of their work and progress, their attitudes to the experience and the attitudes of recipients.

McIvor found that offenders given community service were predominantly young, male, single and unemployed. They had settled living arrangements and had few problems related to alcohol or drugs. Their offences were mainly dishonesty, violence and public disorder. They had an average of five previous convictions and about one-third had been in prison. These findings accord largely with official criminal statistics.

Eighty-five per cent completed their order satisfactorily. Those breached had repeatedly failed to attend. They had more convictions than average and were more likely to have been on probation or sent to prison in the past. They were more likely to have been in group than agency placements but that probably reflected the fact that riskier offenders would be allocated to groups anyway.

Offenders themselves had no clear preference for group or agency placements but unskilled practical work was viewed as the least rewarding. The most rewarding placements were those that brought the offender into contact with recipients, where new skills were developed and where the benefits to the recipient were apparent. Overall, offenders were very positive about community service.

There was a very similar picture from recipients, over 90 per cent of whom were satisfied with their experience of community service. There were a few complaints about unreliability, poor supervision and shoddy work but almost no problems related to the fact that those doing the work were offenders (for example, only one incident of theft from a recipient was reported).

A small sample of 134 offenders was followed for reconvictions for four years after completion of orders. After two years, 57 per cent had been reconvicted and after four years 66 per cent had been reconvicted. Reconviction rates tended to be slower than prior to the order and were for less serious offences. Those most likely to be reconvicted were those with the most past offences and/or the most problems. Those who had particularly good experiences of community service appeared to be less likely to be reconvicted.

McIvor concludes:

The CS order may not have lived up to initial hopes that it would make a significant contribution to reducing the reliance of courts upon the use of custodial sentences. It is, however, a less costly option than imprisonment, one which many offenders find to be rewarding and worthwhile and one which appears to be no less effective than other court disposals in reducing recidivism. In most cases . . . it is highly valued [by those] who have been the recipients of unpaid work.
(McIvor 1992:188)

Women and community service

There is nothing in theory or in law to debar women from doing community service but sentencers have always had ambivalent feelings about giving such orders to women. It has always been viewed by courts as not quite appropriate. The chivalrous view is that it isn't quite nice for ladies to be doing such hard work and that probation is much better for all but the most hardened of them. The practicalities of availability have also always been an obstacle – the absence of childcare facilities is the main problem – though the fact that it is a much greater problem if the woman goes to prison tends to be overlooked. Occasionally a magistrate will express a paradoxical view which is simultaneously enlightened and paternalistic:

Community service is usually done in someone's spare time – women don't have any!
(Magistrate quoted in Worrall 1990/1995:65)

It would be gratifying to think that this view was an expression of a deeper concern about the justice of requiring society's largest group of unpaid workers to perform even more 'voluntary' work as punishment (Dominelli 1984).

Within the probation service there are also concerns about finding appropriate work and supervision for such small numbers. What is meant by appropriate work? Should women be encouraged to broaden their horizons and do 'male' work or should they stick to what they know in order to ensure they get through the hours?

Overall,[1] about 5 per cent of female offenders receive community service orders, compared with 9 per cent of male offenders (Worrall 1996a). The difference, however, is even more significant in the age range 17–20, where 14 per cent of men receive orders, compared with 6 per cent of women. As Hine (1993) points out, the most pertinent question to ask of these figures may not relate to the low level of sentencing women but to the high level of sentencing men. Community service, it could be argued, is permeated with the ideology that it is a 'young man's punishment'.

Hine also identifies greater inconsistency in the use of community service for women than for men. Using elements of the Cambridgeshire Offender Gravity Rating, she found that while two-thirds of the men on community service in her study were convicted of 'mid-range' offences and had 'mid-range' criminal histories, this applied to only a half of the women. Hine concludes:

> that there is less consensus for female offenders on community service, which suggests that factors other than offence and previous criminal history played a greater part in their sentencing than it did for male offenders.
>
> (Hine 1993:69)

In a later article, Hine and Thomas (1995) express concern about the increasing proportion of first offenders among women placed on community service (a rise from 18 per cent in 1981 to 30 per cent in 1991, compared with 10 and 13 per cent respectively for men).

This concern is reflected in Barker's (1993) investigation of the attitudes and experiences of women serving community service orders. For one-third of the 48 women she interviewed, this sentence represented their first contact with the criminal justice system. For most of the women interviewed, community service had been an enjoyable and worthwhile experience, despite difficulties in organising childcare. Criticism is levelled at probation officers who, in the majority of cases, did not argue well for community service in pre-sentence reports (and this study, it must be remembered, was concerned with women who *had* received such orders). Barker is optimistic about the future of community service for women, arguing that, as numbers increase following the 1991 Criminal Justice Act, some of the problems identified will resolve themselves. Her study, however, significantly omits interviews with women who are experiencing difficulty in completing orders or who have been subject to breach proceedings. Armstrong (1990), for example, paints a more pessimistic picture of women's completion rates and lays greater emphasis on the sexual harassment some women experience, especially when placed in predominantly male work groups. It is a matter of regret that Barker's badly needed research, funded by the Association of Chief

Officers of Probation, should have to be completed, as it appears to have been, under severe time constraints. Despite this, the study provides useful data to support the view that community service can, and should, be used more frequently to keep more women out of prison.

Restorative justice or punishment of the body?

The relationship between work and punishment is highly complex. It has long been recognised that rates of imprisonment fluctuate in correlation with unemployment rates and, more broadly, that punishment responds to the needs of capitalism, though the exact nature and dynamics of that relationship remain contested (Box 1987; Howe 1994). The position of community service within that discourse has never been examined seriously. Indeed, the silence can only be described as wilful, since any serious attempt to theorise the role of community service would almost certainly unearth some very uncomfortable explanations for its popularity and persistence. Far better to leave well alone, it might be argued, than to unsettle the foundations of one of the few penal success stories of the latter part of the century.

That is undoubtedly the tone adopted in *Paying Back: Twenty Years of Community Service* (Whitfield and Scott 1993). Pease and McWilliams' (1977) indicators of change have been absorbed into the culture of community service and the picture presented in the book is predominantly one of a visionary penal innovation founded and developed on the theory of restorative justice. The potential for reconciliation between the offender and the community is the book's unifying theme. The collection is unashamedly celebratory and includes nine pages of sunny photographs of schemes, offenders and recipients. One has to search for critical perspectives, but Oldfield's chapter on 'lost opportunities' strikes a more sombre note. He reminds us that community service has made little impact on the use of imprisonment by courts, has encouraged net-widening and may even have 'enabled a smoother transition towards the "justice" model . . . with the emphasis in future likely to be on creating more punitively interventive disposals' (Whitfield and Scott 1993:30). Community service, he argues, has become an *accompaniment* to imprisonment, not an alternative to it.

Foucault (1977) has established in our consciousness the recognition of a distinction between (historical) state punishment as the deliberate infliction of pain on the human body and (modern) disciplinary state punishment, where the object of penalty is 'the soul' – the thoughts, will and inclinations – of the criminal. As such, the soul is susceptible to 'scientific knowledge' – to a whole set of assessments, diagnoses and normative judgements made by psychiatric, pedagogic and social-work experts. The purpose of the project is to produce docile, obedient bodies by focusing attention on the 'mind' of the offender. The battle for the mind of the offender, as we shall see in Chapter 8, has been fought primarily between those experts who base their knowledge claims on psychoanalysis and psychotherapy, and those who are collectively termed cognitive behaviourists. Whichever school we ascribe to, Foucault has forever reordered our understanding of the development of penal analysis into that of the relationship between power, knowledge and the body (Smart 1983).

But what is the knowledge that underpins community service as a penal intervention? What 'expert' assessment and classification is required in order socially to construct an offender as 'suitable' to be punished by work? What model or theory of offending is invoked to support a recommendation that an offender should be 'sentenced to serve' (McIvor 1992)? The whole point about assessment for suitability for community service is that it is based on the criteria of 'fitness to work'. We know that those most likely to be placed on community service are fit young men and, since most criminals are fit young men, that is perhaps what we would expect. But all other forms of punishment either take no account of youth and fitness (for example, fines and conditional discharges) or they are imposed despite youth and fitness (as with prison and probation) because other factors are considered more important (for example, the offender's dangerousness or personal problems). Community service is the only punishment specifically designed for fit young men. All other offenders are judged suitable only to the extent that they display the same characteristics as fit young men. Those who do not meet the criteria are not always excluded but they are always seen as requiring 'special' provision, as being Other than a 'proper' community service offender. Thus women and those with health problems or disabilities have to be treated differently and always represent the compromise, the concession – not the authentic article.

The authentic article, then, is he who can and, therefore, should work to regain his citizenship. This may be all very well in times of full employment, when it is only the sick or the criminal who do not work. In such times, the symbolic and practical value of community service is clear. The three R's – reparation, restoration and reintegration – may succeed in dignifying the voluntary efforts of the offender. There is no need to worry too much about the degree of pain inflicted on the body. 'Honest sweat' is the lot of every worker – there is nothing essentially different about work done by an offender.

But what happens in times of recession and high unemployment? When honest work is at a premium, how do we make sense of work as punishment? When working for nothing ceases to be exculpatory of itself and is seen instead as a reward for wrong-doing, it makes only limited sense to talk of reparation, and no sense at all to talk of restoration and reintegration. Teaching offenders to be disciplined, skilled workers in times of unemployment is not merely irrelevant but may even present a threat to the honest unemployed. The spectre of 'less eligibility' looms again.

It could be argued, therefore, that the lasting appeal of community service has very little to do with civilised notions of restorative justice. It has far more to do with a return to Foucault's punishment of the body:

> But a punishment like forced labour or even imprisonment – mere loss of liberty – has never functioned without a certain additional element of punishment that certainly concerns the body itself: rationing of food, sexual deprivation, corporal punishment, solitary confinement. (Foucault 1977:15–16)

That is not yet a recognisable description of community service, though we only have to look to the reintroduction of the chain gang in Alabama to see how easily it could become so. Suggestions are made regularly that offenders should wear emblazoned tabards and that most placements should involve hard physical work. There is little concern here with the 'soul' of the offender, nor yet with the production of Foucault's docile obedient bodies. What lurks here is the desire for spectacle. Prison keeps the really dangerous offender out of sight and our twentieth-century sensibilities require us to turn away in embarrassment from inadequate or mentally disordered offenders receiving their treatment. But watching healthy, fit young men being physically humiliated may be the nearest we will get to the hanging, drawing and quartering of Foucault's shocking opening pages (1977).

A footnote on attendance centres

Of all non-custodial disposals, the attendance centre order has been the most neglected in the literature and it has been difficult to know how to include it in this book. Attendance centre orders have been available for juvenile and young adult offenders since 1948 and have retained their popularity with sentencers, with 15 per cent of juveniles being so sentenced in a recent study of the Youth Court (O'Mahony and Haines 1996). Originally intended to punish by deprivation of leisure time, the order's similarity with community service has been pointed out (Gelsthorpe and Tutt 1986). Like community service, its objectives are unclear and its flexibility is attractive. It is used across the range of offences (not just for 'football hooligans', as many believe) and appears to float up and down the sentencing 'tariff', being used as both an alternative to custody and to fines or supervision orders. It has the advantage of lacking any strong public image, but is generally regarded favourably because:

> it is run (indirectly) by the police; structured (hours and attendance), and carefully programmed (physical training and constructive hobbies); all these factors have greater appeal ... than the unstructured and less specific arrangements of a supervision order to a social worker. (Gelsthorpe and Tutt 1986:151)

Conclusion

The chameleon-like nature of community service has been viewed by many commentators as its strength but it remains a punishment without a knowledge base. It has no philosophy, because it is 'an undisguised attempt to curry favour with everybody' (Wootton cited in Pease 1983:76). Its rationale is unsophisticated and has developed very little, if at all, since its inception. Debate, when it has taken place, has been either around the sterile and positivistic question of whether community service is an alternative to custody or a sentence 'in its own right' – whatever that means – or about the appropriateness (or otherwise) of National Standards, particularly in relation to breach proceedings. The only spark of intellectual challenge has come through discussion about the suitability of community service for women – a discussion which has required community service organisers to examine the nature of the community service 'experience' and what it is meant to achieve. The paucity of intellectual rigour in the analysis of community service has become so entrenched that it is now impossible to find any serious professional or academic commentary on the subject. It is no longer a subject of any interest. Compared with prison, it will always be viewed as a 'soft option' by those on the political right. Liberals will continue to cherish notions of reconciliation and restorative justice, while pragmatists will see it as a mechanism for damage limitation and the management of criminal careers – the forestalling or delaying of eventual incarceration. Community service, it seems, just *is*. It requires no justification, no case to be made out for its legitimacy. It can be whatever we want it to be. It is the complacent face of Punishment in the Community.

Note

Pages 96–97 are reproduced by kind permission of Jessica Kingsley Publishers from G. McIvor (1996) *Working with Offenders*, Research Highlights in Social Work 26.

CHAPTER 8

From counselling to instruction: the development of 'help' in probation discourse

Introduction

Much work with offenders, both individually and in groups in centres, is now based on cognitive behaviourism (a version of behaviour therapy which is ethically less messy than the *Clockwork Orange* version (Burgess 1962) and more easily appropriated by semi-experts in the probation service). 'Advise, assist and befriend' has given way to 'confront offending behaviour'. Changing the whole personality through insight-giving, or changing the offender's environment through welfare assistance are no longer seen as feasible goals. Instead, the focus is much narrower, less ambitious. What needs to be changed are particular pieces of unacceptable behaviour – no more and no less. And, ironically, this is seen as being less intrusive, more respectful of the offender 'as a whole person'. From McGuire and Priestley's ground-breaking book *Offending Behaviour: Skills and Stratagems for Going Straight* (1985) to Ross and Fabiano's *Reasoning and Rehabilitation* programme (1989) the battle is now on for the 'mind' of the offender – or, at least, for those bits of the minds of particular (young, unemployed, male) offenders that most frighten respectable citizens.

The aim of this chapter is to examine the changing theoretical underpinnings of the 'help' offered by the probation service, the move away from psychotherapeutic approaches towards behavioural approaches and the resulting political and ethical dilemmas. In order to do this, the chapter is divided into two distinctive sections. The first considers the development of the physical settings in which 'help' is offered; the second explores the changing nature of the 'help'.

The first section will begin by considering the development of probation (day) centres providing programmes of normalising instruction to compulsorily attending groups of offenders in increasingly lavish purpose-built buildings as the visible representation of Punishment in the Community in the 1980s and 1990s. The partial restriction of liberty involved in these programmes provides an ideal 'last resort' sentence before imprisonment for serious and recidivist offenders. Yet the numbers of offenders passing through centres are minute in comparison with those sent to prison and centres struggle to justify their existence. At the same time, probation hostels, which have a less glamorous tradition, continue to be regarded as the 'Cinderella' of service provision (White 1984), despite their ability to cater for some of the most basic needs of offenders.

What are probation centres?

A probation centre is a building approved by the Secretary of State and run by the probation service to provide programmes of organised activities for offenders made subject to probation orders with requirements to attend such programmes. Under the Criminal Justice Act 1991, a probation order requiring attendance at a centre is a community sentence which meets the sentencing aim of restricting an offender's liberty. It is normally used for serious offences which are close to being serious enough to warrant imprisonment. Offenders are normally required to attend for up to 60 days and if they fail to do so may be subject to breach proceedings.

The first centres (known initially as day training centres and later as day centres) were established in 1973. In the past, some centres admitted offenders on a voluntary basis but most programmes are now confined to offenders on court orders. Most activities in centres are for groups of offenders and they range from being intensively therapeutic (for example, work with sex offenders) to providing constructive leisure pursuits. Offenders are expected to 'address their offending behaviour' which means accepting responsibility for, and facing up to the consequences of their actions, trying to understand why they commit offences and looking for realistic ways to stop offending. Offenders also receive help with personal problems affecting their offending and learn social skills to improve the way they function in their daily lives (including such things as adult literacy, assertiveness training, anger management and alcohol education).

Most probation centres are attended predominantly by young white men, who constitute the majority of serious offenders coming before the courts. In accordance with anti-discriminatory practice, there is concern that better provision should be made for black people and women in order that centres are perceived by other probation officers and by sentencers as being appropriate disposals, thus avoiding custodial sentences for these offenders.

When courts make a probation order, it is open to them to make specific additional requirements and they do so in about one-quarter of all orders. The most significant additional requirements concern medical (that is, psychiatric) treatment, residence, attendance at a probation centre for a certain number of days and participation in specified activities, often, though not necessarily, at a probation centre. Out of a total of about 49,000 probation orders made in 1994, 6,600 included 'specified activity' requirements and this represented an increase from 2 per cent of all orders in 1985 to 13 per cent in 1994. Numbers required to attend a centre full-time, however, declined from 3,100 in 1990 to 2,800 in 1994 – a mere 5 per cent of all orders (Home Office 1996b). A particular experiment, funded by the Home Office and entitled 'intensive probation' eventually catered for fewer than 800 young adult offenders in eight schemes over a two-year period (Mair *et al.* 1994).

The history of probation day centres

The emergence of probation day centres is usually associated with the prison crisis of the early 1980s, the search for tough alternatives to custody and the drift towards greater surveillance and control of offenders. One of the earliest examples usually cited is that of the Kent Close Support and Probation Control Unit which operated from 1979 to 1984 and catered for both juvenile and adult offenders (Vass 1990). The regimes consisted of highly structured days and evening curfews, monitored by random home visits. The Unit was intended as an alternative to custody for serious offenders and was very controversial. But that is not the whole story. The first four official day centres, set up in Sheffield, Pontypridd, Liverpool and London, following the 1972 Criminal Justice Act, were clearly designed to provide training in social and personal skills to 'the socially inadequate petty recidivist' (Vass 1990:136).

The demise of the rehabilitative ideal in its classical individualised form stimulated a search among liberal and radical probation officers for alternative forms of therapeutic work. The 1970s saw an increased interest in groupwork of various kinds, ranging from prisoners' wives groups to groups for juveniles and groups for those unemployed or homeless offenders who tended to 'camp' in probation office reception areas. Provided participation was voluntary, groupwork was viewed by many as a means of reducing the stigma of individualised work, facilitating self-help and mutual aid and redressing the unequal power relationship of 'one-to-one' work. In short, it was seen as a more democratic way of working with offenders (Senior 1985).

But groupwork presented a very practical problem to probation officers – space. Few probation offices had rooms large enough to cater for a group (which would be a minimum of six to eight people) in any comfort. Some had meeting rooms or staff rooms but these were viewed as 'no go' areas for clients and conflicts arose when some probation officers tried to negotiate for their use by groups. Some use was made of local community facilities but this involved fees to hire rooms and the inconvenience of transporting equipment and people. Groupwork was not for the faint-hearted and, since it tended to be regarded by management as an optional extra, only the most committed and enthusiastic became involved. And when key personnel left or transferred to other offices, groups folded very quickly, thus losing much of their credibility with staff and clients alike.

All this resulted in what Mair has called the 'garden gnome' syndrome

(1995). Summarised less humorously than in the original paper, this syndrome occurs when a probation officer wakes up one morning, decides she wants a new challenge and recalls that there have been a disproportionate number of garden-gnome thefts in the locality recently. She decides to set up a group for garden-gnome thieves and becomes an expert. Word gets around and soon every area is 'discovering' a need for groups for garden-gnome thieves. By the time the Home Office gets to hear, such groups are springing up all over the place, with a variety of different approaches, presenting a problem of co-ordination. The point of the fable is that such *ad hoc* developments demonstrate 'uncontrolled discretion, lack of accountability, reinvention of the wheel, flavour-of-the-monthism . . . inefficiency and ineffectiveness' (Mair 1995:254).

One way to establish the centrality and legitimacy of groupwork in relation to service resources was to raise its profile with sentencers. Making attendance at groups a condition of a probation order would ensure an appropriate allocation of resources and would enable such work to be taken more seriously by courts and the service itself. During the late 1970s, such conditions were included increasingly on an *ad hoc* basis but proved controversial on grounds of civil liberties. By 1982 the practice was successfully challenged in the Court of Appeal in the *Cullen* v. *Rogers* case. Subsequently, provision was added to the 1982 Criminal Justice Act in Schedule XI, making it legal for attendance conditions of up to 60 days to be included in probation orders. There were technical differences between Schedule XI 4(A) and 4(B) conditions, the former being rather more flexible in their application than the latter, but these distinctions need not trouble a present-day reader too much.

What actually goes on in day centres?

What actually goes on in day centres has been viewed with suspicion from the outset. This is partly because it has never been entirely clear what purpose they serve. In a succinct and enlightening article written in 1982, Anne Howe and her colleagues pose the kind of questions which many were asking about this new sentencing 'toy':

> consider whether you are doing things *to* offenders, *for* them, or *with* them . . .
> Are day centres about meeting client need or about changing Probation practice?
> With self-referral, people attend because they want to, because day centres are welcoming places and users can see their personal problems responded to. They also keep people off the streets and overcome loneliness. Day centres are complex systems, organic and changing. Structure irons out uncertainties but it may discriminate against some users.   (Howe *et al.* 1982:60–61)

The debate about voluntarism and compulsion continued throughout the 1980s (e.g. McLoone, Oulds and Morris 1987; Scarborough, Geraghty and Loffhagen 1987; Owen and Morris-Jones 1988) and represented the focusing of a wider and more fundamental debate about care versus control on to a particular (and literally) concrete setting. The debate also affected the content of day centre programmes. Achieving a balance between structured activities aimed directly at addressing offending behaviour and those aimed more at enhancing self-esteem and developing personal and social skills was not easy. It also became apparent that there were limits on the levels of participation that could be required of someone whose attendance was compulsory. Offenders could be compelled to attend and sit in a room with an instructor or trainer. But they could not be compelled to talk about themselves and certainly not to discuss any problems or behaviour which they might consider intimate or confidential. That could only be done voluntarily, whatever the court might say. So any notion of 'therapy' or 'treatment' had to be ejected from day centre discourse and programmes tended to fall into three broad categories:

1   *Educational* programmes, such as alcohol education, health education, literacy and numeracy, victim awareness, drugs education, job-seekers' clubs, debt management and so on;
2   *Leisure-control* programmes, designed to develop new constructive leisure skills, such as art, drama, sport and so on; and
3   *Cognitive-behaviour* programmes, designed to enable offenders to identify and modify visible behaviour which was seen to cause problems to other people and which may or may not cause problems to the offender.

Each of these categories presented ethical dilemmas, though relatively minor ones in the first two instances. Anything described as 'educational' immediately poses the problem of 'how people learn' and it was apparent that, in the early years, enthusiastic probation officers with no training as teachers sometimes became disheartened by the lack of response among their 'pupils', especially those juveniles who could not tolerate anything that reminded them of school. The spectre of 'less eligibility' also raised its head. Why should offenders have special education and extra help in finding jobs and accommodation when law-abiding folk cannot get such help?

A similar criticism was levelled at 'leisure' activities. Arguments about self-esteem and the constructive use of time were not well received by a public having to pay more and more for their own leisure activities.

But by far the most difficult ethical minefield was the third category of activity. In order to compel participation in behaviour modification without invoking cries of 'treatment without consent!' probation officers had to construct the behaviour in question within a specific discourse in order to establish legitimacy for the programmes concerned. This will be considered in greater detail later in this chapter, but suffice to say at present that the behaviour had to be constructed as being:

• Specific and bounded – not some generalised personality trait;
• Illegal and not just anti-social;

- Victim-creating or potentially victim-creating and not just a problem to the offender;
- Controllable by the offender and therefore a matter of choice; and
- Capable of being corrected without recourse to medical or psychological expertise.

Consequently, such programmes became known as 'offending behaviour groups' or 'offence-focused groups' to make clear that no attempt was being made to change either the personality of the offender or their social circumstances. On the one hand, it could be argued that this offered some protection to the offender against overly intrusive therapeutic intervention. On the other, however, it allowed probation officers to abrogate responsibility for treating the offender as a 'whole person' in a social context.

The 'bible' used by probation officers in day centres during the 1980s was McGuire and Priestley's (1985) *Offending Behaviour*, which is packed with accessible 'pen and paper' exercises and innumerable training ideas to interest offenders in the potential rewards of *not* committing crimes. The tightly argued introductory chapter sets out a theoretically sound framework for their approach, emphasising the importance of voluntary participation by offenders and of placing the work under the control of the offender, rather than the 'therapist'. There is no place, it is argued, for behaviour-change methods that involve the manipulation of forces *external* to the offender. But this section of the book was invariably ignored by hard-pressed workers who all too frequently simply 'dipped' into it five minutes before a session was due to start to look for 'something to do'. Also ignored was the final chapter entitled 'Beyond the Individual', which argued the limitations of individual work and the need for social change and penal reform. The book went as far as recommending the decriminalisation of prostitution, possessing cannabis, drunkenness and even unlawful sexual intercourse where the offender and victim are of similar age (1985:209). It was indeed a radical book but, ripped from its proper context, McGuire and Priestley's work all too often became a caricature.

Probation centres and discrimination

Probation (day) centres have always been male-dominated environments. Mair's national survey (1988) found that 95 per cent of those attending were male. This means that, as with community service, a vicious circle of male-orientated provision exists whereby probation officers are reluctant to recommend such orders because of the poor provision and those working in centres blame the absence of recommendations for the inadequate provision (Armstrong 1990). The picture is further complicated, as we saw in Chapter 6, by officers' fears that they may be colluding with discrimination if they recommend for a probation centre order a woman who seems to have an insufficiently hefty criminal record to warrant it (Dunkley 1992).

Women, of course, are not excluded from centres and there are many laudable examples of women-only groups being run (Mistry 1989; Carlen 1990; Buchanan, Collet and McMullan 1991; Jones *et al.* 1991). All too often, however, women have had to fit in with existing male-dominated groups. Including a lone woman in a male group, for example, on alcohol education, highlights the problem. Images of drunken women are very different from images of drunken men (McConville 1983) and stereotyped judgements (including those from other group members) may prove particularly intimidating for a woman in that situation. Not only is she unlikely to benefit from the experience of the group but she may well be rendered more vulnerable to breach proceedings if she feels she cannot face the situation. Such arguments are well-understood within the probation service but the practice persists nevertheless.

Provision for black and other ethnic minority offenders in centres is even more inadequate, except in a few notable areas such as the Black Groups Initiative in the Inner London Probation Service (Lawrence 1995).

The 1992 National Standards were strangely quiet about probation centres and the 1995 version is completely silent.

Probation hostels

The probation service has a long history of partnership with charities and voluntary organisations in the provision of accommodation for young boys and girls (Le Mesurier 1935) but approved hostels for adults have only existed since 1973 (White 1984). Their development coincided with a broader concern about the impact of homelessness or poor accommodation on recidivism. Their aim was to provide probation clients with stable accommodation and sufficient support to complete their probation orders without reoffending. It was assumed that most would be employed or could be helped to find a job with the appropriate support and encouragement. Liaison with local Housing Departments often meant that permanent accommodation could be found after about 12 months in a hostel.

By the 1980s, however, the situation had changed considerably (HM Inspectorate of Probation 1993). There was a shortage of traditionally 'suitable' hostel residents and under-occupancy became a problem. In 1991 the average rate of occupancy was just under 75 per cent. With high levels of unemployment and the demand for provision to keep more serious offenders out of prison, especially while on remand between court appearances, the probation hostel became less of a roof over one's head and more of a house of correction in its own right.

The hostel experience of the 1990s has been very much about providing 'a high restriction of liberty . . . in a structured and supervised setting' (HMI 1993:13). National Standards make clear that it is not intended for minor offenders, nor for those 'whose sole need is accommodation' (HMI 1993:21). Hostels are required to be selective in their admissions, rejecting anyone whose offence is 'too minor', who might harm staff or other residents or, conversely, might be vulnerable to harm by other residents (Home Office 1995e). Similarly, strict rules are to be applied prohibiting disruptive or offensive language, as well as violent or abusive behaviour. All this is quite reasonable in theory, and one would hope that most residents could be helped to reach such a standard of civilised conduct through the hostel experience. But it has meant that those most in need of the support provided by hostels are increasingly excluded because of the high standards they are required to reach *before* admission.

Hostels have also suffered from a lack of status within the probation service. Although wardens are qualified probation officers, the remaining staff are not. Indeed, working as an assistant warden is recognised as a stepping-stone for those wishing to enter training. Consequently, many stay in one hostel for only a year or so, in order to gain the minimum required experience.

Despite these concerns, it could be argued that the probation service – or rather NAPO – has shot itself in the foot in relation to hostels. Following the 1991 Criminal Justice Act, the Home Office announced plans to increase the number of bail hostel places (admittedly with a view to privatising some of the provision) in line with the Act's stated intention of reducing the remand population in prison. In response, NAPO began industrial action in 1992 against 'unsafe' staffing levels in many hostels (NAPO 1992). This involved members boycotting referrals to hostels that were deemed unsafe, with the result that in 1993 occupancy levels dropped to an all-time low. Although the dispute was settled in the same year, the additional NIMBY factor (Not In My Back Yard) meant that the planned expansion met with much local resistance and much of the money allocated by the Home Office remained unspent (NAPO 1993). Hostels, it seemed, were becoming too troublesome an issue. In April 1994 the Home Office closed 11 bail hostels, involving the loss of 270 places or 10 per cent of overall provision (NAPO 1994). Despite steady increases in the prison remand population, five more hostels were due to be closed during 1996 (NAPO 1996).

Probation hostels and discrimination

In 1991, a total of 878 offenders received probation orders with conditions of residence (HMI 1993). Of these, almost 97 per cent were male and more than half were aged under 21. Hostel provision for women is woefully inadequate, with only three all-women hostels in the country – in London, Birmingham and Liverpool. Of these, only one caters for women with children (although another mixed hostel also has facilities). Forty-six other hostels make some provision for women but this often amounts to one or two beds in an otherwise male-dominated hostel (Wincup 1996). In such situations it is recognised that it is difficult 'to create a sense of safety and privacy for women without simultaneously suggesting a feeling of entrapment' (HMI 1993:45). Consequently, some hostels decide that it is not worth the trouble of accommodating women, thus reducing the number of available places overall and involving women in travelling long distances away from their home areas. In these circumstances, it is perhaps not surprising that 'demand' for female hostel places appears low, while the female prison population continues to rise. Woolf and Tumim's recommendation (1991) for small-unit community prisons for women, allowing greater access to community provision, was derided by women's campaigners at the time, but, in the present penal climate, it now looks like a missed opportunity to improve the overall stock of supervised accommodation for women (Hayman 1996).

Hostel provision for black and other ethnic minority offenders is also inadequate but for slightly different reasons. The Commission for Racial Equality has argued against separate provision for black people (HMI 1993) but hostels are still seen as 'white institutions'. As in other areas of anti-discriminatory practice, hostel staff are cautious about making any claims that they are successfully catering for black residents. Nevertheless, this laudable introspection results in more and more black people being sent to prison.

Having examined those physical settings, outside the traditional office, in which 'help' is offered by the probation service, we now turn to an examination of the nature of that 'help'.

The development of counselling in probation

The role of counselling in probation has always been ambiguous. Historically, the exhortation to 'advise, assist and befriend' was more closely associated with the duties of citizenship than with professional skills and knowledge. Probation officers in the early part of the century were viewed as being somewhat avuncular – upright citizens offering wayward youths the benefit of their experience within a relationship of benevolent authority.

Such work fitted well with Edwin Sutherland's theory of differential association (Taylor, Walton and Young 1972). Crime, like all social behaviour, is learned from those with whom one associates most closely. The extent and nature of the influence of a relationship will depend on its duration, its intensity and its importance to the person concerned. In the same way, law-abiding behaviour can be learned from wholesome relationships. As Le Mesurier says:

> The probationer may come to look on his probation officer in a new light, respect ripen into friendship, and the foundations be laid for a lasting relationship, the nature and influence of which will be evident after personal contact is no longer possible.
> (Le Mesurier 1935:129)

Unfortunately, Le Mesurier spoils this warm picture by reminding the probation officer that it is difficult to cultivate such relationships when ten or twenty probationers are reporting in one evening! Nearly 50 years later Walker and Beaumont (1981) quantify the point by arguing that probation officers spend on average only 2.1 hours a month with each probationer.

After the Second World War, however, much greater emphasis was placed on psychodynamic and, later, Rogerian approaches to counselling (Williams 1996b), which required probation officers to develop particular interviewing skills and to work within a framework of social work values.

Psychodynamic approaches are, broadly speaking, concerned with what is 'hidden' and in particular with conflict that is hidden. Behaviour is viewed as a manifestation, expression or symptom of an underlying unresolved conflict. That unconscious conflict causes conscious anxiety which is managed through defence mechanisms such as repression, projection, splitting, denial, reaction formation and so on. Such mechanisms serve to bolster and protect a fragile and falsely positive self-image. At the root of the conflict are relationships between individuals and significant others, between the past and the present, between inner and outer reality. A key theme is that of *transference*, whereby an individual behaves towards another individual as though they were someone else in their life. An example might be the offender who treats their probation officer as though they were a parent or a son or daughter, thus engaging in inappropriate interaction. Related to that is the notion of *counter-transference* – for example, the similarly inappropriate feelings which an offender may invoke in the worker. The resolution of conflict comes through its conscious acknowledgement and acceptance, and the task of the worker as expert is to identify the source of the conflict and make that knowledge accessible to the client (Coulshed 1988; Lishman 1991).

Probably the most well-known articulation of these skills and values can be found in a book called *The Casework Relationship* by Felix Biestek (1961) which set out seven principles of 'casework':

Individualization is the recognition and understanding of each client's unique qualities and the differential use of principles and methods in assisting each toward a better adjustment. Individualization is based upon the right of human beings to be individuals and to be treated not just as *a* human being but as *this* human being with his personal differences.   (p.25)

Purposeful expression of feelings is the recognition of the client's need to express his feelings freely, especially his negative feelings. The caseworker listens purposefully, neither discouraging nor condemning the expression of these feelings, sometimes even actively stimulating and encouraging them when they are therapeutically useful as a part of the casework service.   (p.35)

The controlled emotional involvement is the caseworker's sensitivity to the client's feelings, an understanding of their meaning, and a purposeful response to the client's feelings.   (p.50)

Acceptance is a principle of action wherein the caseworker perceives and deals with the client as he really is, including his strengths and weaknesses, his congenial and uncongenial qualities, his positive and negative feelings, his constructive and destructive attitudes and behaviour, maintaining all the while a sense of the client's innate dignity and personal worth.   (p.72)

The non-judgmental attitude is a quality of the casework relationship; it is based on a conviction that the casework function excludes assigning guilt or innocence, or degree of client responsibility for the causation of the problems or needs, but does include making evaluative judgments about the attitudes, standards or actions of the client.   (p.90)

The principle of client self-determination is the practical recognition of the right and need of clients to freedom in making their own choices and decisions in the casework process. Caseworkers have a corresponding duty to respect that right, recognize that need, stimulate and help to activate that potential for self-direction by helping the client to see and use the available and appropriate resources of the community and of his own personality. The client's right to self-determination, however, is limited by the client's capacity for positive and constructive decision-making, by the framework of civil and moral law and by the function of the agency.   (p.103)

Confidentiality is the preservation of secret information concerning the client which is disclosed in the professional relationship. Confidentiality is based upon a basic right of the client; it is an ethical obligation of the caseworker and is necessary for effective casework service. The client's right, however, is not absolute.   (p.121)

These principles have been set out at length because they are often wilfully misunderstood by those who wish to decry 'casework'. Although some of the language is dated, there is little here to which most probation officers could take exception in the routine of their work. The feasibility of casework within a probation setting has always been questioned, however, because of the authority vested in probation officers to return offenders to court (Walker and Beaumont 1981). The problem may not be quite as acute as in America:

Usually, the counselor [*sic*] carries a badge that enables him or her to arrest and incarcerate offenders. The counselor may carry handcuffs, leg and body chains, electronic surveillance bracelets, and even firearms . . . [S]ome authorities are of the opinion that effective counseling relationships cannot be developed under such conditions.   (Masters 1994:13)

Nevertheless, the likelihood of achieving genuine changes of attitude and behaviour in an offender under these conditions is justifiably viewed with some scepticism. By the 1970s, many probation officers saw traditional counselling as patronising and oppressive, designed to encourage clients to accept their place in the community and their lot in life (Raynor 1978).

The demise of the rehabilitative ideal outlined in previous chapters resulted in radical approaches to counselling which focused on the potential of groups to raise client consciousness of common problems and their social, rather than individual, causes. Groups were seen to provide mutual aid and self-help, and to redress the balance of power in the professional–

client relationship. But they offered no immediate evidence of reducing recidivism and, as such, gained little credibility with management and the courts, who demanded more visible evidence of success)

Behavioural approaches to the 'treatment' of offenders had been of only peripheral interest to probation officers, mainly because of the levels of medical expertise required but also because of the ethical dilemmas posed by methods that were apparently applied without the informed consent of the offender/ patient.

Behaviour modification is based on the belief that behaviour is learned through a process of stimulus and response. This may be done in one of two ways. Respondent (Pavlovian) conditioning is concerned with behaviour over which we may have little control, such as physical reflexes, sexual arousal, anxiety, fear and anger. It is relevant when considering specific inappropriate learned behaviours such as phobias, addictions or violent sexual behaviour. Here the key to understanding is that the client has made an inappropriate connection or association between a stimulus and a response. In a mild form, this is the basis on which advertising works. For example, a man may be sexually aroused by a picture of a scantily clad woman sitting on a sports car. Subsequently, driving fast cars may become a sexually arousing activity. There is no need for a Freudian explanation – the behaviour has been learned through association. In order to change the behaviour, it is necessary to break the connection – in working with phobic conditions techniques of *desensitisation* (introducing the patient gradually to the feared experience) or *flooding* (overwhelming them in such a way that their fear reaction fails to function) may be employed to help a client control a fear reaction; in working with addictions (including sex offending) *aversion* techniques may be used so that the association becomes unpleasant rather than pleasurable. But such work tends to be specialised and is not often appropriate for probation officers unless it is very closely supervised in institutions by psychiatrists or psychologists.

Of more use on a day-to-day basis is operant (Skinnerian) conditioning which emphasises the importance of *consequences* as reinforcers of behaviour. Much use is made of the ABC model:

A = Antecedents = Stimulus
B = Behaviour = Response
C = Consequences = New Stimulus

In operant conditioning the initial response (B) may be random or experimental: for example, a child throwing her first tantrum when refused sweets or a teenager committing his first theft. Whether or not that response becomes a learned piece of behaviour will depend on the consequences (does the mother give in and provide sweets? Is the teenager caught?). Patterns of behaviour depend not so much on the original stimulus (lost in the mists of time) but on how present consequences reinforce present responses (Coulshed 1988; Lishman 1991).

In order to change (or shape) behaviour, the aim is to change the consequences by either increasing or decreasing the positive reinforcers (or rewards), depending on whether the behaviour is to be encouraged or discouraged. This might be done through modelling (behaving in the desired way to show the client the good consequences), contracts (agreeing rewards for behaviour changes), points systems or time out (physical removal from the source of reward) – or simply by praising and withholding praise. It is important to note here that punishment (the infliction of physical or emotional pain) should have no part in this form of behaviour modification for at least three reasons:

1   It doesn't help the person to learn new good behaviour;
2   It can have serious side-effects of depression or copying (negative modelling);
3   People learn to tolerate punishment.

Cognitive behavioural work is based on operant conditioning but accepts that, unlike animals, humans are not just creatures of physical response. We are 'reflexive'. Intervening between stimulus and response is our perception of a situation. Our responses are shaped by our beliefs and thoughts about reality. Those beliefs and thoughts may be distorted when viewed objectively by other people (for example, a sex offender may *believe* that a five-year-old child is being seductive) but they have real influence in shaping our response to a stimulus. Changing our thought processes – the way we assess situations mentally – will change our responses in the same way as more physical or emotional rewards.

Cognitive behavioural approaches have become very popular within the probation service for all the reasons outlined earlier in this chapter. They have also provided the rhetorical link between discourses of 'help' and managerialism. One of the three sacred words in managerialism is 'effectiveness' and we can now turn to the ways in which the concept of 'effectiveness' has been incorporated into the helping project through the use of cognitive behavioural work.

What works? The effectiveness debate

The traditional measure of effectiveness in the probation service has been the correlation between report recommendations and sentencing decisions. As Raynor, Smith and Vanstone (1994) have said, when probation officers talk about effectiveness they tend to refer to their success in diverting offenders from custody. Reconviction rates have never been of great interest, especially after the court order has ended. Probation officers feel that they cannot be held responsible if an offender reoffends 12 months after a probation order has finished. If an offender navigates the order itself without reoffending, then that is considered sufficient success.

But Raynor, Smith and Vanstone suggest that it ought to be possible to steer a middle course, which identifies indicators of effectiveness other than crude reconviction rates but which nevertheless allows probation officers to assess their effectiveness in helping an offender to reform. These 'broader measures of success' (1994:78–84) are:

- Anti-poverty strategies, which establish networks of information and support to help offenders deal more successfully with official agencies concerned with benefits and employment;
- Anti-oppressive practice, which ensures equality of treatment for black people and women and equality of access to appropriate provision inside and outside the probation service;
- Drug misuse and harm reduction work;
- Accommodation strategies;
- Reduction of harm caused by the criminal justice system, by continuing to influence sentencers and seeking to divert as many offenders as possible from custody; and
- Reduction of harm caused to victims of crime, by assisting victim support schemes and increasing victim awareness among offenders.

There is no 'quick fix' to make people stop committing crime. Nothing can guarantee reform but all these measures will affect offenders' attitudes and behaviour, making it more likely and thus offering the greatest hope of long-term protection for the public.

We saw in Chapter 2 that Robert Martinson's (1974) pronouncement that 'nothing works' helped to accelerate the loss of confidence in rehabilitative measures and although he made a partial retraction in 1979, the legacy of disillusion persisted. In the late 1980s and early 1990s, however, a new mood of optimism accompanied the 'discovery' of cognitive behavioural approaches and a series of conferences entitled 'What works?' were held to encourage evaluative research and its dissemination. In the forefront of this movement was James McGuire (of McGuire and Priestley fame) and his encouragement has given new impetus to the probation service to experiment in its work with offenders.

STOP and TURAS

Two examples of programmes that claim to 'work' are reported on in consecutive chapters of James McGuire's latest collection (1995a). A comparison of the two programmes demonstrates both the diversity of imaginative work being undertaken by the probation service *and* some significant differences of principle which are, it might be argued, not superficial.

Straight Thinking on Probation (Raynor 1992; Raynor and Vanstone 1994; Knott 1995) is a programme run by the Mid-Glamorgan Probation Service, based on the 'Reasoning and Rehabilitation' programme developed in Canada by Ross and Fabiano. The programme consists of 35 sessions, each two hours long, held twice a week. The programme is delivered by probation officers as part of a 'specified activities' condition of a probation order. The sessions take place in the probation centre.

The programme employs methods of cognitive training: it aims to develop offenders' thinking skills and thus increase their range of problem-solving options. The programme claims to 'teach offenders':

- Self-control;
- Thinking skills;
- Social skills;
- Values, enhancement;
- Victim awareness;
- Creative thinking;
- Critical reasoning;
- Social perspective taking;
- Their effect on others;
- Emotional management;
- Helper therapy (setting up situations where the offender is in the role of helper rather than being helped, thus increasing self-esteem).

Central to the effective delivery of the programme is the concept of 'programme integrity'. This means that the complete programme has to be delivered without amendment or alteration in exactly the way it was conceived by its creators. This appears to have presented the probation officers with some problems since they were not easily convinced that a programme designed for use in Ottawa would necessarily translate directly for use in South Wales (Knott 1995). Nevertheless, fidelity was ensured by scrutinising and monitoring videotapes of sessions and discussing them in supervision. Despite this, three-quarters of participating staff found the experience of running the groups positive (Raynor 1992). Pitts' vision of 'package delivery' appears to be fairly accurate:

the image of Postman Pat going about his uncontentious, and socially useful job, with a smile on his face and a cheery word for everyone.   (Pitts 1992b:143)

The STOP programme was evaluated by Peter Raynor and Maurice Vanstone and appears to indicate a favourable reconviction rate for those who complete the programme in comparison with those dealt with in other ways by the courts, although Raynor and Vanstone are the first to point out the tentative nature of the figures. Qualitative evaluation was also undertaken in the form of interviews with staff and offenders. Almost all the offenders believed that the programme had helped them to make positive changes to their thought processes. Examples provided by Raynor, Smith and Vanstone (1994) illustrate the willingness of offenders to think more carefully about their actions, to 'work things out', to 'look at my options' and so on. However, when asked how this change had come about (Raynor 1992), the quality and quantity of contact with probation officers was very high on the list, as well as the actual programme content and the experience of working together with others.

Success seemed to lie as much in the greater commitment and enthusiasm of the officers (by comparison with 'ordinary' probation) as with the content of the programme itself. As Trotter rather quaintly puts it, reporting on a study of intensive supervision of offenders in Australia, 'numerous studies . . . have suggested that the adoption of a pro-social approach by supervising officers is related to reduced recidivism' (1995:237). John Hagan (1994) calls it 'investment' in social and cultural capital – an idea we examined in more detail in Chapter 4.

The STOP programme seems to have had some limited success, arguably despite its adherence to 'programme integrity', compulsory attendance, and an overtly educational, classroom approach. It can be criticised for its social and political neutrality, although Raynor, Smith and Vanstone attempt to argue that it does improve people's social circumstances because it gives them more options in tackling their difficulties – for example, greater skills in negotiating with officialdom.

TURAS, the Irish word for 'journey', is more openly subversive in its philosophy. A probation programme for car thieves or 'joyriders' in Belfast, it challenges the pessimism of 'underclass' theorists. Chapman (1995) believes that government policy has had a vested interest in maintaining an excluded class of young people who can be blamed for the ills of society while being contained by a 'cordon sanitaire' (see Jones 1983) which prevents them from interfering with those who benefit from existing social conditions. Creating a culture of constructive change among these oppressed minorities threatens the *status quo* which prefers to see problems managed rather than solved.

The philosophy of TURAS is faithfully translated into a practice which owes more to 1960s community work than to 1990s punishment in the community. Recruitment to the programme is done through outreach work involving home visits and street-corner work. This is a far cry from court orders which make programmes compulsory conditions of probation orders. But there is more. Once contact has been made, activities are organised at times when offences are most likely to occur. This involves go-karting from midnight to 3 am, drop-in centres open until 2 am, standing on street corners all night and taking young people to late-night restaurants! Moreover, there is no attempt at this stage to 'confront offending behaviour'. The purpose is merely(?) to develop trust, break down communication barriers and get to know the young people. Only after all this groundwork are offenders recruited to the formal courses and subsequent personal development plans.

As with the STOP programme, reconviction rates are encouraging, but the programme itself has clearly become a respected feature of the local community, making a greater contribution to its sense of well-being than any narrow statistical objectives would indicate. As Chapman concludes, 'essentially the programme is about growing up, a task that society makes increasingly difficult, particularly for young men' (1995:137).

Conclusion

At present there is a great danger in thinking that the 'What works?' framework is *the* solution. Advocates of reasoning and rehabilitation work emphasise the importance of programme integrity. This may seem a reasonable requirement if the programme is to be evaluated and we have seen the problems that arise when workers use material out of context. But such rigidity smacks of mystification and imperialism. After all, the TURAS programme probably would not work very well in Birmingham, unless account was taken of the very different racial and political context. As Pitts argues, 'effective rehabilitation ventures are reflexive rather than directive . . . successful interventions do not seem to travel well' (1992b:144). The danger of resisting the pessimism of 'nothing works' is that it is replaced by equally hollow rhetoric. We know that 'something works' or that 'some things work', but the circumstances under which some things work, for some people, some of the time, need to be researched honestly and sensitively, without recourse to meaningless soundbites that serve only as feeble rejoinders to the dominant discourse – that of 'prison works'.

CHAPTER 9

Unacceptable crimes or unacceptable criminals? Sex offenders

Introduction

The following two chapters will illustrate the changing attitudes to offenders outlined above, using sex offenders and juvenile delinquents as case studies. These two categories of offenders are not usually put together but the juxtaposition here is deliberate. Both the sex offender and the young offender have undergone a significant reconstruction within official discourse on crime and disorder. Both have been demonised but both (albeit in very different ways) have epitomised the contradictions that result from policies based on an inadequate understanding of the complexities of the issues involved. Sex offenders are constructed simultaneously as 'strangers' and 'known', as 'monsters' and 'ordinary blokes', but always as lying and manipulative recidivists. Young offenders are constructed simultaneously as 'just boys being boys [*sic*]' and 'little monsters', as 'growing out of crime' and being 'persistent offenders' but always as (ir)responsible offenders against society rather than as victims of its failures. And there are young sex offenders (Richardson 1990). Juveniles account for approximately 7 per cent of all convictions for sexual offences, up to 85 per cent of whom may have been victims of sexual abuse themselves (James and Neil 1996).

Sex offenders – monsters or ordinary blokes?

The change of public and governmental attitude towards sex offenders has forced the probation service to examine the value base of its work. Under attack have been the key concepts of social work value discourse which have traditionally governed the attitudes of probation officers. It is no longer deemed appropriate to exhibit 'acceptance', 'empathy' or a 'non-judgemental attitude' in relation to sex offenders. Indeed, the sex offender is no longer regarded as the 'client':

I, along with many probation officers, find myself helping to justify the use of confrontational methods by recasting my client to be a past and potential future victim rather than the perpetrator in front of me.   (Gocke 1995:175)

Work is based on the assumption that the offender is lying, that he has offended more frequently than he admits and that no mitigation (even his own past experience of abuse) can excuse or even account for his present behaviour. Ironically, feminist analysis has been far more eagerly embraced in work with sex offenders than it has in relation to the treatment of women offenders.

Sex offenders have been increasingly a focus of attention by the criminal justice system over the past decade (Prison Reform Trust 1990b). During the 1980s the police and courts were criticised for failing to take a serious enough view of sexual assault and rape. Following a guideline judgement from the Appeal Court in 1986 (*R* v. *Billam*) custodial sentences increased in length. There was also increased public concern about child sexual abuse, culminating in the Butler–Schloss inquiry in Cleveland in 1987. More offenders were charged and convicted and more were sent to prison. In 1979 20 per cent of sex offenders received custodial sentences; by 1989 the proportion had increased to 33 per cent. The impact on the prison population was considerable. In 1979 4.7 per cent of the prison population were sex offenders, in 1989 the proportion was 7.5 per cent. The trend was set to continue. In 1992, 39 per cent of sex offenders were sent to prison and this was accompanied by a reduction in the number of sex offenders being fined, from 39 per cent in 1982 to 17 per cent in 1992 (Hebenton and Thomas 1996).

The Criminal Justice Act 1991, which originally attempted to reduce the prison population, made an exception in respect of violent and sexual offenders, who could be imprisoned for a longer term than might otherwise be justified in order to protect the public from serious harm. By 1996, attitudes had hardened further. In the White Paper *Protecting the Public* (Home Office 1996a), the Home Secretary proposed automatic life sentences for those who repeat serious sexual offences and also suggested the registration of sex offenders in the community, requiring them by law to notify the police of any changes of address and prohibiting them from seeking employment which involves access to children.

Probation officers find themselves working with sex offenders in a number of different contexts. They may prepare pre-sentence reports in which they are required to make judgements about the risk to the public of not imprisoning the offender. Officers who are seconded to prisons may work jointly with prison officers on the Sex Offender Treatment Programme which is run in selected prisons. More often, they are responsible for the statutory supervision of sex offenders following their release from a prison sentence. Finally, they may provide treatment programmes in probation centres for offenders placed on probation. The numbers of sex offenders placed on probation has remained consistently low: between 12 per cent and 15 per cent of all those convicted and about 2 per cent of all offenders placed on probation (974 in 1994). Numbers placed on community service have been negligible (140 in 1994) (Home Office 1996b).

In all these contexts, probation officers are given a more specific responsibility in relation to the law-abiding community than is expected of them in relation to other offenders. It is officially acknowledged that 'the concern for victims is a distinctive feature of work with sex offenders and one which has wide repercussions for this strategy as a whole' (Sanders and Senior 1994:84).

This is particularly true where the victim is a child and work is governed by the provisions of Schedule 1 of the Children and Young Person Act 1933. In this case, probation officers share with Social Services Departments and the police a duty to monitor the offender if he begins (or returns) to live with a family or in a place where he has substantial access to children. Information about an offender, which would normally remain confidential, becomes inter-agency property in the name of protecting the public.

Knowledge about sex offenders is increasingly being seen as a community's right (Hebenton and Thomas 1996). In America, arrangements for 'tracking' sex offenders are widespread and have repeatedly withstood legal challenges that they constitute cruel and unusual punishment. In England, the issue gained momentum in early 1997, when a council official faced disciplinary action for allegedly alerting mothers on a Birmingham housing estate that a sex offender, recently released from prison, was moving on to the estate (*Independent*, 9 January 1997). One local authority, Middlesburgh, apparently announced that it was formally excluding sex offenders from its housing estates. A forensic psychologist attempted to argue that this might not actually be the best way to protect children because (a) children are more likely to be abused by family and friends than by strangers; and (b) that if sex offenders are not rehoused, they are more likely to become nomadic in their habits, losing contact with supervisors and drifting back into crime. But knowledge has become a matter of business, with consumers and producers. Knowing about the activities of sex offenders is packaged as a prerequisite to preventing their reoffending. In reality, however, it provides the opportunity to profile, classify and stigmatise offenders in the name of risk assessment. Because sex offences are, quite rightly, regarded as extremely serious, there appear to be no ethical constraints on the ways in which the very few sex offenders who are apprehended are allowed to be treated. As Hebenton and Thomas reflect, these ethical issues have not been subject to any scrutiny:

Is compulsory self-accusation, where the offender effectively 'carries a sign in public' admitting to being a moral pariah appropriate?

(Hebenton and Thomas 1996:109)

Who are sex offenders?

A number of laws cover sexual offences and a distinction is usually made between offenders against adults and offenders against children. Offenders are usually categorised as familial child abusers, non-familial child abusers, rapists/indecent assaulters and indecent exposers. The latter are normally still considered to be pathetic rather than dangerous but some feminists argue that the impact of such offences on their victims remains underestimated (McNeill 1987). It is also now part of the received wisdom of sex-offender work that 'flashers' will progress to commit more serious offences unless checked.

It is generally believed that most sex offenders are not mentally ill, in the sense of having a diagnosable, psychiatric illness. Many of those prosecuted are regarded as having personality disorders but victim surveys suggest that offenders come from all socio-economic groups and that many offences go unreported. The attrition rate for sexual offences reported to the police and those which result in conviction is extraordinarily high (Sampson 1994). Therefore, the public image of the sex offender tends to be based on what may be untypical cases. The emphasis on 'stranger danger' is misplaced for two reasons: first, because most victims know their attacker and second, because they are not 'strange' – they are very 'normal' people.

Most sexual offences are committed by men on women but we must not forget that young men and boys can be victims and that a small percentage of abusers are women – official estimates are between 1 and 2 per cent. Female sexual abuse of children is almost certainly under-reported but at the same time is extremely difficult to define since mothers are socially permitted to be far more intimate with their children than are men. There is very little research in this area, though some of the earliest work was done in Styal prison (Barnett, Corder and Jehu 1990). The limited research that is available suggests that some women offenders are coerced into abuse by male accomplices or that the women themselves have been abused as children by men (Welldon 1996). The debate about the extent of sexual abuse by women has been characterised by what Forbes (1992) has called 'the search for equivalence'. Forbes argues that the 'discovery' of female sexual abusers represents a reassertion of a 'gender-free' analysis of child sexual abuse, which deflects attention from the centrality of male oppression in physical and sexual abuse. The creation of a moral panic about women's participation and collusion in sexual abuse is just one more example of the ways in which women are blamed for the behaviour of men.

Images of sex offenders

Attitudes towards sex offenders are highly ambivalent. When a 13-year-old 'rape beast' was found to be too young to be sent to custody because of a legal loophole (closed by the 1994 Criminal Justice and Public Order Act), the newspapers were outraged, despite the less-than-convincing circumstances surrounding the conviction (*Daily Star*, 12 November 1994). The fact that the boy was 'half-caste' and 'lives with his mother' (*Today*, 12 November 1994) undoubtedly fuelled the hyperbole about sons of the underclass. By comparison, Austen Donnellan, a 21-year-old university student, who might be expected to know better, received nothing but sympathy and support from the papers when he was acquitted of rape. Date rape is, after all, a phenomenon which threatens us all – men and women – because it challenges the games and rituals we all use in our relationships with the opposite sex. It makes us realise how vulnerable we all are and how easy it is to misread signs and to make mistakes. But the particular issue which infuriated the papers in this case was the anonymity rule which allowed the alleged victim – but not the alleged perpetrator – to remain unnamed. 'Shouldn't she now be named?' screamed the *Daily Mail* (20 October 1993) in a bid to punish the woman who, as a consequence of the acquittal, became retrospectively constructed as a false accuser. Similar indignation accompanied the acquittals in 1995 of Michael Seear, a policeman, and Craig Charles, a well-known television actor.

The same analysis can be applied to notorious child sexual abuse cases. Myths about peculiar practices on remote islands underpinned the press reporting of the Orkney case but 'ordinary blokes' were falsely accused by an obsessive and irrational female doctor in Cleveland (Campbell 1988). In both cases, ultimately, the rights of children to protection (but from whom? their parents or the system?) were sacrificed to the fears of adults (Asquith 1993). Feelings of disgust and revulsion are mixed with the terror of the false accusation. Sex offenders have to be seen as 'not like us' – as monsters, beasts, perverts – definitely not 'ordinary blokes'.

The construction of the monster is also influenced by racism. Just under half of all adult male sex offenders are convicted of rape (as opposed to child sex abuse) but that figure masks a more alarming statistical comparison. Just over one-third of white sex offenders are rapists, while 80 per cent of black sex offenders are convicted of rape. The myth of the black rapist serves not only to sustain and legitimise racial oppression but also to hinder the theorising of rape. On the one hand, reliance on official statistics suggests that rape is disproportionately committed by black men. On the other, working with black sex offenders in a way which is confrontative but not oppressive presents a dilemma for probation officers (Cowburn and Modi 1995). Challenging a black sex offender's denial of guilt exposes a worker to accusations of racism.

What happens to those convicted?

One-third of all sex offenders go immediately to prison and that proportion increases to 75 per cent in the Crown Court. Traditionally, sex offenders or 'nonces' are the lowest form of life in prison and are placed on Rule 43 or segregation for their own protection. More recently, with increased numbers, special units called Vulnerable Prisoner Units have developed to allow a more constructive and humane regime away from other prisoners. Grendon Underwood prison has traditionally been the only prison to actively 'treat' sex offenders: the regime is based very much on the lines of a therapeutic community with a psychotherapeutic approach (Genders and Player 1995).

An alternative, which was used in the 1960s and more in America than Britain, was behavioural therapy which attempted in a direct and physical way to force offenders to unlearn deviant behaviour, through aversion therapy, covert sensitisation and masturbatory reconditioning. Apart from prompting the kind of ethical objections highlighted by the book and film *A Clockwork Orange* (Burgess 1962), the other concern about such techniques was their inability to address the motivation which activated and sustained sex offenders or to provide offenders with any insight into their behaviour (Barker 1995).

In recent years, however, a cognitive behavioural approach has become very fashionable both inside prisons and among probation officers who run treatment groups for sex offenders – either for those not sent to prison or those released from it.

The basis of this work is to challenge offenders' distorted thoughts and reasoning in relation to their victims and to help them manage their impulses by providing alternative courses of action which they view as being more rewarding. The work is based on the belief that, in order to commit a sexual offence, the offender has to overcome both internal and external inhibitions as well as the victim's resistance. He therefore has to convince himself that he is doing no harm (or that the victim deserves it) or release his inhibitions through drink or drugs. He has to manipulate the environment to make the offence possible and he has to groom the victim in order to reduce her resistance. All this takes careful planning. Hence the refusal by workers to accept the claim that the offence was committed on impulse. It is assumed that offenders have committed several offences before they are caught and that any denial is lying. The offender is not allowed to deny either the facts or the impact of his offending. Every attempt to justify or excuse his offence is challenged. He is not allowed to blame his victim in any way. Instead he is put deliberately under pressure to discuss the offence in detail and admit that it was a matter of choice – that other choices were possible. A well-established ABC routine is followed, whereby the offender is helped to unlearn and relearn appropriate sexual behaviour by considering in detail the antecedents of the offence (A), the behaviour engaged in (B) and the consequences for himself and the victim (C).

The early evidence is that such programmes are effective to the extent that recidivism rates appear to be reduced among those treated as compared to those untreated or treated in other sorts of programmes (Barker 1995; Hedderman and Sugg 1996). It is necessary, however, to select offenders carefully. Child abusers appear to respond better than rapists, perhaps because the latter find it harder to accept full responsibility for their actions in our 'rape-supportive culture' (Burt 1980 cited in Gocke 1995). Longer programmes are, perhaps predictably, more effective than short ones and programmes which teach offenders techniques which they can utilise themselves, especially to prevent relapse, are also successful. Finally, the quality and management of the staff involved is crucial to the effectiveness of the programme. As Gocke, among many others, has pointed out, working with sex offenders is often a stressful and stigmatised activity in itself:

> For periods of time I operate apparently untouched by the horror and despair of the details of the offending and how it relates to my own male attitudes and values, concentrating instead on the process of intervention. However, at fairly regular intervals this is pierced by an issue or an instance which brings out the sheer awfulness of the situation, leaving me upset, angry, depressed and self-doubting.   (Gocke 1995:177)

Workers less sensitive and reflective (and qualified) than Gocke may not manage their personal feelings so well. Waite (1994) is scathing about the poor training given to prison and prison probation officers in preparation for becoming tutors on the Sex Offender Treatment Programmes in prisons.

But there are other ethical dilemmas. First, the treatment is still concerned primarily with the unacceptable behaviour – it is less concerned with more fundamental belief systems. The offender is encouraged to replace an illegal response to his sexual arousal with a legal one. He may still retain what we may consider to be unacceptable views about women and children and be unrepentant about his desire to have power over them. Second, the way in which the treatment is conducted may amount to little more than 'legitimized nonce-bashing' (Sheath 1990). It may be a legitimate way for prison officers and probation officers to 'have a go' at sex offenders by verbally humiliating them. It is also argued that this may be counter-productive because it puts offenders on the defensive and they learn to give the required responses without genuinely exploring their feelings and problems.

Practices of exclusion and strategies of intervention

Despite our knowledge that sex offending is widespread and under-reported, official discourse constructs sex offenders in a very specific way, on the basis of those who are convicted in the courts. Such an offender typically has a history of (often undetected) minor sex offending which escalates to the more serious. Once established, that pattern of offending persists for years unless checked. The offending is rarely impulsive and involves planning and the manipulation of people. The offender is skilled at denying the seriousness of his offence and at manipulating others into colluding with his denial (Home Office 1996a). Any other attempt to describe or account for the life and behaviour of the offender is constructed as Other and excluded from legitimated discourse. Anyone who challenges this construction risks being accused of collusion, unless the alleged perpetrator is black, in which case it is acknowledged that there may be a lack of fit between anti-racist values and the values underpinning work with sex offenders (Cowburn and Modi 1995).

The debate on working with sex offenders in the community has been virtually foreclosed. The field of intervention has been exploited to its maximum but, despite evaluation studies that indicate grounds for cautious optimism (Barker 1995), official government discourse now rejects the language of rehabilitation in favour of the language of surveillance and control through information. The probation service has no alternative discourse with which to challenge this shift because it has itself accepted the official construction of the sex offender. It has sacrificed its better judgement about why people offend and what makes them stop, based on decades of accumulated wisdom, but has found that it no longer matters (to the public, the media or the government) whether or not it delivers in terms of preventing recidivism. The sex offender has been constructed as irredeemable. It is no longer his crimes that are unacceptable; he himself is unacceptable as a member of the community. He is forever non-reintegratable.

CHAPTER 10

Unacceptable crimes or unacceptable criminals? Juvenile developments

Introduction

The development of the 'growing out of crime' or 'systems management' approach to juvenile justice during the 1980s has been generally acknowledged to have been a penal success story. Traditional tensions between 'justice' and 'welfare' models lessened as a multi-agency approach attempted to combine the best of both worlds in order to reduce the numbers of young offenders being imprisoned at the same time as resisting net-widening among pre-delinquent youngsters. But the myth of the 'hard core' of dangerous and/or persistent young offenders was tenacious and the murder of Jamie Bulger 'proved' that the 'stunted little man' – the prematurely worldly wise artful dodger identified by Matthew Davenport Hill in 1855 and cited in Pearson 1983 – is still dangerously alive and well in the 1990s.

In his book *Hooligan: a History of Respectable Fears,* Pearson (1983) traces back, generation by generation, the fears which respectable middle- and upper-class people have had about the dangerousness of young people. The middle-aged and old are always bemoaning the behaviour of the young and harking back to a golden age – about 30 years ago – which, of course, never existed. Pearson shows how public fears have always been fuelled by the media and how the stereotyped explanations of juvenile crime have been remarkably similar throughout the generations.

Such explanations always start with a typification of the 'British' (or should it be English?) way of life as one of natural domestic peace. Disorder, it is argued, is alien to English life and can only be explained by foreign influence. Every generation has had its own particular form of racism whereby it has blamed youthful disorder on (currently) black people and previously, Americans (during and after the Second World War), Irish people (the original hooligans of the early twentieth century), Mediterranean people (the mid-Victorian garrotters) and Arabs (as in 'street arabs').

Additionally, youth crime is then attributed to any combination of the following:

- Lack of authority in the home (weak fathers);
- Lack of affection in the home (working mothers);
- Lack of discipline and moral teaching in school;

- Popular entertainment (ranging from street festivals and the theatre to football and television); and
- Unbridled freedom and luxury (as a result of the perceived increasing affluence of every younger generation).

And all this is mirrored and reinforced by a system of law and justice which is too lenient.

It is against this backcloth of constant public fear about the uncontrolled independence of youth – and the reality that something like a half of all crime is committed by people under the age of 20 – that the development of the juvenile, and latterly youth, justice system in England has to be seen.

Three questions underlie all debates about youth crime. First, how far can young people be held responsible for their criminal actions? Second, in a civilised society, how far should the welfare of a young person take precedence over the requirement to punish? Third, how can we prevent this troublesome youth from growing into a dangerous adult? In attempting to answer these questions, the history of juvenile justice has been one of a pendulum swinging between neo-classical ('justice') arguments and positivist ('welfare') arguments.

The history of juvenile justice

Until the middle of the nineteenth century both adults and children were subject to the same laws and penalties, including prison, hanging and flogging. It is true that, in law, children under 14 were presumed to be incapable of committing a crime (*doli incapax*) but for children over seven it was possible and usual to rebut that principle so that children as young as that could be, and were, hanged for trivial offences.

In the early and mid-nineteenth century there was increasing concern about the crime and disorder supposedly resulting from the industrialisation and urbanisation of a rising (and therefore predominantly young) population (Gillis 1974). Early capitalism favoured young people because it increased their earning power. But it also separated them from their homes and families, making them independent, affluent and undisciplined. To this was added a fear of the growing socialism and social protest in Europe (the Chartist movement in England). The mixture was seen as lethal.

Official discourse began to categorise the vulnerable poor as belonging to either the dangerous or the perishing classes – the former being actively dishonest and disobedient, the latter being feckless and susceptible to contamination by the former. The distinction is an important one because it has persisted throughout the history of juvenile justice in various forms; namely, the depraved and the deprived, the delinquent and the neglected, the child in need of care or protection and the child in need of control.

Saving some children

The treatment of juvenile offenders in the nineteenth century provides a case study of the development of criminological thought from classical theory, through neo-classical theory to positivism. Reducing harsh penalties on the young and improving the living conditions of the poor were compatible with neo-classical thought but the development of the *reformatory movement* and later the *child-saving movement* falls squarely into the terrain of positivism.

It was recognised that the appalling conditions of child labour and the breaking of family ties had contributed much to a premature ageing of children and that they needed to be rescued, separated and protected. Thus adolescence was discovered, or created.

The delinquent is a little stunted man already – he knows much and a great deal too much of what is called life – he can take care of his own immediate interests. He is self-reliant, he has so long directed or misdirected his own actions and has so little trust in those about him, that he submits to no control and asks for no protection. He has consequently much to unlearn – he has to be turned again into a child.
    (Matthew Davenport Hill, 1855, 'Practical Suggestions to the Founders of
                                            Reformatory Schools' cited in Pearson 1983: 167)

The model for the reformatory movement was that of the public school and with it a middle-class ideology of childhood and adolescence which involved parents – or parental substitutes – in responsibility for and supervision of the activities of their children. Under the banner of democracy and classlessness the lifestyle and ideology of the middle classes was imposed on the 'honest working classes' as the norm. Those working-class parents who could not or would not supervise their children were required to give them up to the state. Delinquent children were sent to reformatory school while vagrant, begging or neglected children were sent to industrial schools. The reformatory system was based on the assumption that proper training can counteract the impositions of poor family life, a corrupt environment and poverty, while also toughening and preparing delinquents for the struggle ahead.

By the end of the nineteenth century, the reformatory movement had given way to what has been called the *child-saving* movement (which started in America but had its equivalents in this country) (Platt 1969). It was dominated by middle-class women advocating what have been termed 'maternal values' and seeking to re-establish the virtues of the home at a time when industrialisation threatened this. The most important feature which distinguished this from earlier reforming movements was the increasing focus on *the whole child* and on *all children*. Significantly, the distinction between reformatory and industrial schools lapsed and children in trouble were consolidated into a single conceptual category: the depraved and the deprived were one and the same. 'Couched in the language of welfare and supported by an army of professionals, attention was continually diverted from what children *do* to what children *are*' (Morris *et al.* 1980). Adolescence became an object of scientific observation and clinical treatment. What began as an attempt to protect adolescents against the decadent world of adults ended in imposing a new conformity sanctioned by positivist social science and separating them from their civil and social rights.

Regulating all children

The assumption now underlying work with young people was that all children were potential delinquents. Crime appeared to be rising but much of that was because of the extension of the criminalisation process. More and more borderline anti-social behaviour (such as gambling, loitering, begging, dangerous play, malicious mischief and 'care and protection' situations) was being brought before the courts. 'Every boy and girl . . . had in them a bit of the street arab' (Gillis 1974:174). Crime was no longer a matter of free will or moral voluntarism. Rather it was a matter of psychological determinism. So punishment had to be replaced by prevention and control – and the earlier the better. Signs of criminality could be picked up early enough but this required constant vigilance. So it was no longer only a matter of separating out and institutionalising certain children, but rather of regulating all youthful activity, either indirectly through the parental authority of good parents assisted by the school and organised gender-appropriate youth clubs (like Scouts and Guides) or directly through the state's professional mothers – who later became social workers!

In the early twentieth century, the welfare approach to juvenile justice was predominant. Following the Gladstone Committee in 1895, an indeterminate, rehabilitative sentence of borstal was introduced in 1900 and a separate juvenile court was established in 1908. The Juvenile Court dealt with both deprived and depraved children and this philosophy was reinforced in the 1933 Children and Young Person Act which stated that the welfare of the child must be the prime consideration. Magistrates in Juvenile Courts were required to have special interest in children and restrictions were introduced on reporting cases. The terms 'conviction' and 'sentence' were removed.

The turning tide

The Children and Young Person Act 1969 was the culmination of the conflict between 'welfare' and 'justice' models of juvenile justice. It attempted to decriminalise and depoliticise juvenile justice. The philosophy of treatment was intended to remove the stigma of criminal proceedings from young offenders. The distinction between the delinquent and non-delinquent child in trouble was blurred and the most appropriate people to deal with both were the trained experts – the social workers. And that meant predominantly local authority Social Service Departments rather than the probation service.

But the political tide had already turned and the Act was about five years too late. It was never fully implemented or resourced and the 1970s saw youth crime once again becoming a moral panic and being repoliticised. Cautioning increased as did preventive intermediate treatment schemes but so did custodial sentences, as more and more young people were drawn into the system and, as we saw in Chapter 5, magistrates refused to entrust them to the care of social workers.

As we saw in Chapter 2, during the 1970s, the optimism of the welfare or rehabilitative model, which was dependent on economic and social confidence, came under attack from a number of directions and this had particular implications for work with young offenders. The political right turned the economic recession into a moral crisis and those working with young offenders were increasingly required to demonstrate their ability to control rather than to help them. At the same time the political left accused social workers of unwarranted intrusion into the lives and liberties of young people. Social enquiry reports were seen as unsubstantiated character assassinations which labelled and stigmatised young offenders, making it more likely that they would adopt a deviant identity. Social workers themselves, especially juvenile justice workers, were seen as irresponsible and dangerous empire builders, likely to do more harm than good. Magistrates and lawyers began to argue that 'due process' and common sense offered greater protection to young offenders than did social workers. And all this was set against a background of damning research studies which appeared to show that 'nothing works' and that rehabilitation is unattainable through any formal intervention (Pitts 1990).

But the 1982 Criminal Justice Act was not entirely a backlash. Although it rationalised and strengthened youth custody provision and introduced the 'short, sharp, shock' (three weeks to four months of a regimented regime in a detention centre) it also had to avoid overcrowding in prisons. So it invested a lot of money in intermediate treatment and diversion schemes as alternatives to custody. Consequently, the government attempted to deal with the welfare/justice conflict with a policy of 'bifurcation', making a distinction between the hard core, persistent minority of offenders and the majority who were a tolerable nuisance.

The successful decade

The key turning point came in 1983 when the Department of Health and Social Security issued a circular to local authority Social Service Departments known as the LAC 83(3) Initiative which did three things. First, it moved intermediate treatment away from preventive provision to alternatives to care and custody, moving it up-tariff. Second, it established inter-agency liaison in intermediate treatment provision –

later to be known as 'partnership'. Third, it provided special finances to pump-prime new projects for three years (Nellis 1991).

Social work intervention began to be reserved for those already show- ing signs of being persistent offenders. Juvenile justice workers used their skills to persuade key decision-makers such as the police and magistrates to intervene as little as possible and impose the minimum possible sentence on young offenders. A feature of this attempt to manage the system was 'gatekeeping', or the monitoring of decisions and developing strategies and tactics to influence decisions. To do this, social workers had to offer an 'alternative tariff' of sentences which were seen to be as challenging as custody but less damaging and less expensive. Examples were 'tracking' or intensive surveillance and the use of the 'correctional curriculum'. The latter, based on theories of human motivation, comprises a set of techniques to enable the offender to identify the moments in the behavioural sequence which culminated in the delinquent act, when they might have acted differently. Role-play, cartooning and video feedback encourage the offender to identify key triggers to offending. The programme then desensitises the offender to those stimuli and teaches alternative non-criminal responses. It is not necessary in either tracking or the correctional curriculum to understand or help the young person – their welfare is not a central concern, but their offending behaviour is.

The emphasis in New Right politics was the responsibility of the individual; woolly-minded work with groups and communities was no longer acceptable. Social and environmental problems were irrelevant; what mattered was individual behaviour. Behaviourism offered the possibility of a time-limited, highly focused intervention which addressed behaviour which those with the power and authority to penalise wanted to change. It could be quantified and measured and justified to a court.

Facts and figures

So what happened to juvenile crime in the 1980s? Contrary to popular impression, the decade saw a sharp fall in the number of juveniles known to be committing crime. The number of juveniles found guilty or cautioned for indictable offences declined by 34 per cent between 1984 and 1994, from 206,800 to 135,800 (NACRO 1996). That decline far outstripped the 16 per cent fall in the number of juveniles in the general population and was largely consistent across age and gender. Overall, the proportion of crime known to be committed by juveniles declined from 36 per cent in 1984 to 26 per cent in 1994.

Most of the crime committed by juveniles is not particularly serious. In 1994 sexual offences and robbery each accounted for only 1–2 per cent of cautions or convictions for males, with another 11–12 per cent being for crimes of violence. Of the remaining 86–87 per cent the vast majority related to property; more than half were for offences of theft and handling stolen goods. For females, about three-quarters of all offences are theft and handling. Violence accounts for a similar proportion as it does for males but robbery and sexual offences are virtually non-existent (NACRO 1996).

Cautioning increased significantly: in 1979, 50 per cent of all juveniles were cautioned. By 1990 it was 75 per cent for males and 89 per cent for females. This varied with age (higher when younger) and geographical area (85 per cent in Surrey to 44 per cent in Durham). By 1995 the proportions had fallen slightly, especially after Home Office circular 18/1994, which restricted its use. Nevertheless, Home Office research shows that 85 per cent of offenders cautioned do not reoffend. Nor is there much evidence to suggest that large numbers are being repeatedly cautioned (Home Office Statistical Bulletin 16/1996).

Custodial sentences also fell dramatically from a peak of 12,000 in 1984 to 3,600 in 1994 (the figures for girls fluctuated between 50 and 100). The White Paper *Crime, Justice and Protecting the Public* argued that 'there is no evidence that the reduction in the use of custodial sentences has resulted in increases in juvenile crime' (Home Office 1990a:45). It even questioned 'whether it is necessary to keep the sentence of detention in a young offender institution for girls under 18' (1990a:45).

As we saw in Chapter 3, the replacing of the Juvenile Court by the Youth Court was an attempt to reflect the age balance of young offenders brought to court, which was overwhelmingly in the 14 to 17 age group, while younger offenders were being successfully diverted from prosecution. At the same time, however, courts were given the 'flexibility' to impose adult sentences on 16- and 17-year-olds. In other words, the boundaries between youth and adulthood were being blurred, ostensibly to reflect the differing rates of development among adolescents.

A return to Victorian values

Such blurring both reflected and reinforced a perceived desire of public opinion to treat young criminals less and less differently from their adult counterparts. In this, a return to early Victorian values can be detected. Two emergent moral panics of the early 1990s have been joined by a third, more recent, folk devil. 'Rat Boy', the elusive persistent offender who laughed at the system, was soon accompanied by the more awful spectre of 'Child Killer' and now both have been joined by 'Tank Girl' – the new breed of 'feminist' girl criminal.

The 'Growing out of Crime' school (Rutherford 1986) taught us that many young people experiment with offending but most desist as they mature. A smaller group persists to become young adult criminals and an even smaller group commits one very serious offence. By conflating these three distinct groups, the myth is now being created that increasing numbers of juveniles are persistently committing increasing amounts of very serious crime – and increasing numbers of them are girls! We will now examine these three stereotypically constructed juvenile delinquents in more detail.

The persistent young offender

From 1991 onwards, there was increasing concern that a small number of children were committing a disproportionate amount of not-so-trivial crime, especially burglary and criminal damage. Because of their age, they could not be given custodial sentences and the option of being taken into care under section 7(7) of the 1969 Children and Young Person Act had been abolished by the 1989 Children Act. Thus was born the myth of the wild child beyond the control of any authority. Earl Ferrers gave examples to the House of Lords:

There are reports of a 14-year-old from Tyneside who has 28 convictions and who has escaped 22 times from local authority accommodation. Another 14-year-old boy in south London has admitted taking part in more than 1000 burglaries of shops and homes in the past two years . . . He has been arrested 40 times but is too young to be given a custodial sentence for the crimes he has committed. That is pretty hot stuff.   (cited in Morton 1994:2)

In response, in 1992 Michael Howard announced his intention to introduce secure training units for 12- to 14-year-old persistent offenders who were unable or unwilling to respond to supervision in the community. His definition of 'persistent' was the commission of three or more imprisonable offences, one of which must have been committed while under supervision, and the offence under current consideration must be serious enough to warrant a secure training order. In fact, although such children undoubtedly existed, their numbers were far fewer than the government and the media would have the public believe (Hagell and Newburn 1994). Despite this, and despite the very strong professional opposition to his proposals for 'prep schools of crime' (Morton 1994), the Home Secretary proceeded to include this provision in the 1994 Criminal Justice and Public Order Act. The first secure training unit was planned to open its doors in 1997. It is also worth noting that, at the same time, the Home Secretary announced (with no hint of irony) his intention to uncover the full extent of child sexual and physical abuse in local authority children's homes.

Child killers

There has always been an equivalent to a life sentence for juveniles who commit extremely serious offences such as murder, manslaughter and rape. The provision is to be found in section 53 of the 1933 Children and Young Person Act which allows courts to hold juveniles in secure accommodation 'at Her Majesty's Pleasure' and to transfer them to prison when they are old enough. The number of young people, most of them very disturbed youngsters, who have been detained in this way for murder or manslaughter, has fluctuated between 20 and 40 a year for the past 20 years and of these, only 12 in the whole 20 years have been under 14 years of age (Boswell 1996; Cavadino 1996).

What, then, was so very different about Jon Venables and Robert Thompson? Was it the fact that so many adults saw them dragging poor Jamie Bulger to his death and did nothing? Was it the blurred images on the closed circuit TV? Was it the perceived influence of video nasties? Was it just the fact that they were the youngest children to have been convicted of murder? Something about this offence was uniquely postmodern and challenging to our claim to be a civilised society. The veneer of morality seemed to be so easily and publicly stripped away and, despite all the technology, we were still unable to protect a vulnerable toddler from the violence of boys only a few years older than him (Hay 1995). Ever since William Golding's (1960) *Lord of the Flies*, we have had to confront our own knowledge of the depths of depravity that unsupervised boys are capable of, yet the only way in which we seemed able to cope with Jamie Bulger's murder was to pretend that Venables and Thompson had committed an *adult* offence and should therefore be treated like adults, subjected to the full weight of adult sentencing. 'Freaks of Nature' (*Daily Mirror*, 25 November 1993) and 'Evil, Brutal and Cunning' (*Daily Mail*, 25 November 1993) were just two of the screaming headlines that greeted the convictions for murder. The *Sun* asked its readers to fill in a coupon demanding that the Home Secretary increase the boys' sentence tariff (the minimum time they should spend in prison to satisfy the requirements of retribution and deterrence before the authorities consider their rehabilitation) from the 8 years set by the trial judge and the subsequent 10 years set by the Lord Chief Justice. The Home Secretary obliged and set the tariff at 15 years. In 1996 the High Court ruled that this decision was unlawful. The Home Secretary had the right to intervene in setting tariffs for adults but not for children. Children who kill must have their cases regularly reviewed as their personalities develop and mature – something which is inconsistent with a 15-year minimum sentence.

As a result of the Jamie Bulger case, the vexing issue of the age of criminal responsibility was reopened. The four-year zone between 10 and 14 years, when the onus is on the prosecution to produce evidence that a child *knew* that they had committed a serious wrong, was swept away by a High Court ruling in March 1994, though reinstated by the Law Lords a year later (Penal Affairs Consortium 1995).

Tank Girl: the trouble with young women

If we are to believe what we read in the papers then the next moral panic, waiting round the corner, is Tank Girl, a shaven-headed, beer-swilling, feminist superheroine with her biker boots, tattoos, bright red lipstick and 'cocky, feminist, aggressive persona' (Brinkworth 1994)[1]. She and her all-girl gang are menacing the streets, targeting vulnerable women (note the media tactics of divide and rule) who don't expect to be attacked by a group of young girls, some as young as 14 years. But that's not all. These girls may be devious but they are not stupid. They *know*, we are told, that the legal system is soft on them. They *know* how to work it to their advantage, dressing smartly and playing up to the magistrates.

And all this is caused by feminism. This is what happens when you loosen the controls on women. This is what happens when adolescent girls are allowed to think themselves equal or superior to boys. It is every mother's and father's nightmare – their daughter's sexuality rampant and violent. Put succinctly, 'no man is safe'.

Crime is overwhelmingly a masculine activity and the history of juvenile justice and youth social work has been the history of interest in white, working-class young men by white, working and middle-class men. The underlying philosophy has been dominated by ideals of respectable masculinity. The belief that most children grow out of crime if left alone is also based on assumptions about male adolescence: assumptions that crime is an irritating but bearable extension of normal adolescent masculinity – that 'boys will be boys'.

But crime is emphatically not an extension of normal adolescent femininity: it epitomises everything which challenges our expectations of the ways in which 'nice girls' behave. As Lees (1993) points out, the predominant feature of adolescent femininity is walking the tightrope of sexual reputation, avoiding being labelled as either a 'slag' or a 'drag'. It may be true that girls, like boys, will grow out of crime, but the possible damage to their reputations and future life prospects as respectable wives and mothers may be too great to risk radical non-intervention.

Yet our criminal courts are not filled with over-educated, ambitious young women. When girls raise their sights, broaden their horizons, increase their aspirations and self-esteem, they are less likely, not more likely to behave deviantly (James and Thornton 1980). If there is an increase in violent adolescent female delinquency, it is certainly not the result of women's liberation. On the contrary, it has far more to do with certain impoverished young women seeing no future for themselves other than lone parenthood, state dependency and social stigma and saying 'Anything must be better than that.'

The peak age for female offending is now 14 years compared to 18 years for men but at no age does offending by women remotely approach that by men. About one in five known young offenders is female[1]. In numbers that means about 48,000 out of a total of 240,000 (Home Office 1994a). On the whole young women commit less serious crime than young men. They commit proportionately more theft and less burglary (breaking and entering a building). It is true that the second most common crime for young women is violence and its proportionate significance is increasing but we are still talking about only 190 girls (compared with 546 boys) placed on supervision for offences of violence in 1993 (Home Office 1994b).

Although cautioning rates for young offenders are high for both males and females, they are significantly higher for young women – 63 per cent for those under 21, compared with 44 per cent of men in the same age group. This is often attributed to male chivalry and an unwillingness to stigmatise young women with court proceedings. There may also be a belief that young women are more amenable to the shaming process of informal control and that more formal procedures are unnecessary.

By the time they get to court, the proportion of young offenders who are women has reduced to about one in ten. They are more likely than young men to be given a conditional discharge or a supervision/probation order and less likely to be fined or given either an attendance centre or community service order. They are far less likely than young men to receive a custodial sentence. In 1992 only 3 per cent or one in 33 young offenders (excluding fine defaulters) in prison was female (Home Office 1994a). The average prison population of young female offenders was 139, of whom fewer than 10 at any one time were juveniles. That figure represents a steady decline over the previous 10 years and, although the figures crept up again to 245 by late 1996 (National Advisory Council Newsheet Issue 2) this was not out of proportion with the rise in the prison population as a whole at that time.

At first glance, then, it may appear that young women are treated leniently by the system. However, a number of factors hidden by these statistics may cause concern. First, young women appear to be sent to custody for less serious crimes and with fewer previous convictions. Second, young women remanded in custody are only half as likely as young men eventually to receive a custodial sentence. This would appear to imply that, even though the numbers of young women remanded in custody are relatively small, they could safely be reduced further. Finally, in relation to custodial sentences, it has to be noted that 20 per cent of young women in custody are black – a figure out of all proportion to their numbers in the general population – and that increases to 30 per cent for long sentences. The currently accepted explanation for this is that many are drug couriers but that does not by any means account for the whole of the discrepancy between black and white female custody rates.

As for non-custodial sentences, community service and probation (day) centre provision for women is known to be inadequate. Probation officers complain that they receive very few referrals and that it is therefore difficult to make any special provision for women (such as all-female projects or groups). Courts tend to see community service and probation centres as unsuitable for women, both in principle and in practice. So a vicious circle exists whereby the male-orientation of both disposals is perpetuated.

Attendance centres for women are so few and far between as to be fairly irrelevant as disposals for young women (Gelsthorpe and Tutt 1986). So the field of choice is rather restricted. It becomes even more restricted, though, when we look at what has been happening to the probation order and supervision order in relation to juvenile women. The decline of orders made on females has been from 2,200 in 1982 to 583 in 1992. There has been a similar trend in relation to adult women. The current received wisdom is that this decline in the use of 'welfare' disposals is a good thing for women. In the past, it is argued, far too many women have been placed under supervision at early stages of their criminal careers and for minor offences, because they appear to be 'in need' of help. Concern for women's welfare tends to mean concern that they are not fulfilling gender-role expectations and, particularly in the case of young women, concern that they are in 'moral danger', rather than straightforward concern about their likelihood of reoffending. Having been drawn into the criminal justice/welfare net, however, there is a danger that they will escalate up the tariff and into custody. So evidence of a reduction in supervision orders is generally welcomed. Nevertheless, it does raise the question, particularly in relation to young women: if they *are* in need of help, who is going to provide it?

One answer may be found in intermediate treatment which has a very honourable tradition of work with girls. The Cambridge Institute of Criminology *National Survey of Intermediate Treatment* (1990), found that girls accounted for nearly one-quarter of young people involved in the programmes. But they also found that girls tended to be involved at an earlier age than boys and that they were far more likely to be involved in 'preventive' type programmes than in 'alternative to custody or care'-type programmes. Only one-third of the girls were classed as offenders, compared with 80 per cent of the boys.

Standard youth justice thinking (and some feminist thinking) would argue that such provision for girls is discriminatory because it is net-widening and stigmatising. But there is a counter-argument which says that provision for girls in youth work is generally inadequate and that there is a case for what might be termed 'promotional' work with girls to encourage them to realise their potential by providing a supportive female environment in which to explore, through shared experiences, their hopes and fears about their lives.

Despite (or perhaps because of) their small numbers, young women who break the law may encounter discrimination which is both subtle and indirect. But it would be a mistake to imply that formal criminal justice intervention is the most important method of controlling the behaviour of troubled and troublesome girls.

Reporting on her research on the assessment and treatment of young women assessed for local authority care, Annie Hudson says:

Embedded at the heart of contemporary British welfare practice with adolescent girls is an almost psychic fear of a predatory female sexuality. The irony of this should be obvious: it is men who rape and the sexual abuse of children is almost entirely perpetrated by men. Yet, perhaps highest on the professional agenda is the assumption . . . that girls in trouble fundamentally have problems with *their* sexuality.
(Hudson 1989:197)

Many young women who leave home do so because of sexual

exploitation within the family, yet they are expected to want to recreate precisely the same form of oppressive relationships which has served them so badly. All the social, moral and economic pressures on these young women push them towards dependency on men, however feckless and abusive those men might be. At the moment, it seems that all the ills of the world are being laid at the door of 'lone mothers' including responsibility for producing the next generation of young male delinquents. And today's young women in trouble are the next generation of lone mothers, so they need to be watched, controlled and, wherever possible, sent back to the bosom of their families.

All the research that has been done on adult women criminals shows unequivocally that the roots of their criminal careers have lain in the narrowing options of their adolescence. Abuse at home leads to truancy or running away. School exclusion, social workers, residential care, drug-taking and pregnancy narrow the choices even further. Poverty, exploitation and crime lead all too quickly to imprisonment. The stories that have happy endings are always dependent on the slow and often painful re-opening of choice and the associated increase in self-esteem (Eaton 1993).

Conclusion

Although it is true that young people have always been perceived as troublesome by their elders, the assumed relationship between youth and crime seems to be stronger than ever. As Ian Loader (1996) has argued, young people are assumed to be the perpetrators of crime and are rarely constructed as victims or as consumers of criminal justice services. Yet much of the attention paid to young 'trouble-makers' may be due to their inexperience and greater likelihood of detection or to the systematic bias of criminal statistics which emphasise visible and easily counted 'street crimes' rather than the hidden crimes of the workplace and the home (Pearson 1994). In both the latter cases, young people are more likely to be the victims (for example, of employer negligence, sexual assault or child abuse) than the perpetrators.

Juvenile offenders and sex offenders have in common their experience of *exclusion* from the community. Respectable citizens and figures of authority are less and less willing to communicate with either group and are increasingly demanding that they be 'known about', watched and moved on.

Note

1   Pages 135–138 have been reproduced by kind permission of ISTD, King's College London from *Criminal Justice Matters*, No. 19, Spring 1995 pp 6–7.

CHAPTER 11

The future of Punishment in the Community

Introduction

It seems quite clear that nothing is going to change the relentless rise in the prison population towards the year 2000. By late 1996 it stood at just under 58,000 and was rising by 200 to 300 each week. In his 1996 Crime Bill, Michael Howard expected to incarcerate 11,000 more offenders by the year 2011 and planned to build 12 new prisons (*Independent*, 26 October 1996). Mandatory minimum sentences were to be introduced of seven years and three years respectively for third-time drug traffickers and domestic burglars. There were to be automatic life sentences for second serious violent or sexual offences. There was virtually no mention in the Crime Bill of the probation service except in relation to post-release supervision. In the months preceding the General Election of 1997, there was nothing in the manifestos of either of the major political parties to suggest any commitment to less punitive criminal sanctions. Nor is there any prospect of relief from the financial constraints on the probation service. On the contrary, these seem set to worsen (NAPO 1997).

Within this context it is difficult to see the future role of community punishment. Fines will undoubtedly continue to be the main plank of sentencing but it seems unlikely that any further serious attempt will be made to make their imposition fairer. Indeed, new guidelines for fine enforcement were issued to magistrates at the end of 1996. At the same time, however, proposals are being made to introduce community service and electronic tagging as alternatives to custody for 'low level fine defaulters' (NACRO 1996), which may be a welcome move if it does not result in net-widening (for example, where fines might previously have been partially or wholly remitted). Conditional discharges will remain popular for first offenders whose crimes are minor. But that leaves a large space currently occupied by discursively impotent supervisory sentences, all being claimed by their advocates as 'alternatives to custody' and being dismissed by their opponents as 'soft options'. We have lost the sense of graduated response using a range of measures which can be tailored to the needs of those 'middle-range' offenders whose pace of offending needs to be slowed down while they are helped to mature or to resolve the personal and social problems that underlie their offending behaviour. We have been seduced by the concept of 'bifurcation' (Bottoms 1983) and the language of 'seriousness' to view offences as either 'serious' or 'not serious'. We have forgotten that most offences that come before the courts – and most offenders – lie somewhere in between.

Supervision *sans frontières*

It is easy to become obsessed with the problems of criminal justice in England and Wales and this book has not pretended to provide any genuinely international perspective on the issues discussed. Nevertheless, it is perhaps important to set developments in England and Wales in the broader context of developments in other penal systems. Recent analyses have shown that the ambiguities related to 'alternatives to custody' are being experienced by other Western European countries, especially those with previous reputations for liberal penal systems (Sim, Ruggiero and Ryan 1995). Over-emphasis on bifurcation and the simplistic serious/not serious divide has led to a backlash in both Holland (van Swaaningen and de Jonge 1995) and Sweden (Leander 1995) where the public, as in England and Wales, is questioning the definition of 'not serious'. Non-incarcerative measures are increasingly concerned with the restriction of liberty, surveillance and monitoring, rather than with welfare and treatment. The use of 'pure' probation seems to be decreasing everywhere. The attempt to unhitch such measures from prison by making intermediate sanctions sentences 'in their own right' has also had contradictory consequences. No longer seen as 'alternatives to custody' they have become alternatives to each other, thus widening the net of penal intervention – a familiar story.

In France, for example, TIG (the equivalent of community service) is frequently used for first-time car offenders (Gallo 1995) and in Germany alternatives are often used where charges would otherwise have to be dropped through insufficient evidence (Messner and Ruggiero 1995). There is also the danger that the very existence of 'alternatives' reinforces the belief that those in prison *must* be the 'hard core' of offenders and that prison regimes can therefore justifiably reflect this (Leander 1995). But, as van Swaaningen and de Jonge point out, too much criticism of this process serves only to 'vacate the political space to those forces who want to increase the retributive elements' in the non-incarcerative measures, while at the same time alienating probation officers who are struggling to prevent the expansion of the use of prison (1995:39).

A more detailed and comprehensive study of probation around the world is provided by Hamai *et al.* (1995). Across the world, the concept of probation appears to imply four key elements: selection (that is, assessment as suitable); a conditional suspension of punishment (arguably, no longer the case in England and Wales); personal supervision and, finally, guidance or treatment (Hamai *et al.* 1995:4). Beyond that basic definition, probation may mean many different things depending on the social and economic framework within which it has to function. Indeed, one of the authors argues that any attempt to reify or essentialise the concept should be discouraged (Harris 1995).

Comparing the use of probation in England and Wales with other countries, a number of conclusions can be drawn. First, the probation service is probably the largest and most professionalised, with service delivery probably the most coherent and accountable, in the world. In this respect it might still be regarded as 'the envy of the world'. Despite this, or perhaps because of it, it also seems to be the least flexible and most angst-ridden service. Second, it makes less use of volunteers and community facilities than other countries. It seems more conscious of the ambiguities and tensions in the role of probation officer and more concerned about loss of autonomy and professional discretion. In some countries, such as Japan, Canada and the Philippines, volunteers are used extensively and systematically to supervise offenders – a practice which is wholly consistent with notions of reintegration of offenders into the community (Hamai and Ville 1995). Third, the export of a therapeutic model of probation (perceived to be 'British') to developing countries, such as India, has been particularly unsuccessful, partly because of its costliness and partly because of its inappropriateness to resolving the social and economic causes of crime in these countries.

What seems overwhelmingly apparent from this cursory glance at comparative material is that supervision of offenders in conditions of freedom is ineluctably complex and ridden with tensions and contradictions. Attempts to resolve these tensions are doomed to failure and it is a mark of the maturity of a criminal justice system that it can tolerate the ambiguities, recognising the value of flexible and 'floating' penal sanctions which can be used for different reasons with different offenders at different stages in their criminal careers.

Meanwhile, shifting deck chairs on the Titanic...

In the early 1980s the most prominent academic debate about probation was reflected in many articles attempting to reconcile 'care' and 'control'. It was an important debate but one which was overtaken by Home Office intervention and the rise of managerialism in the probation service, as we saw in Chapters 2 and 6. In the mid 1990s a similar academic exercise took place in relation to 'probation values'.

The search for new probation values suited to the 1990s has resulted in both a reworking of the already contested values of 'casework' (see Chapter 8) and an attempt to reconcile the interests of the offender with those of victims and the wider community. Thus Williams (1995) talks about the continuing relevance of 'valuing clients as unique and self-determined individuals' with the capacity to change and with rights to confidentiality. However, the 'community' dimension also involves a greater emphasis on the protection of victims and potential victims. At the same time, Williams argues, there should be opposition to the use of custodial punishments and commitment to equality of opportunity for all. There are obvious dangers (of which Williams is well aware) in producing lists of professional values: they can never be definitive or comprehensive, they are likely to contain contradictory items and they are not exclusive to the profession in question. As such, they are more representative of the ethical agenda of a profession than of any resolution of the dilemmas.

Nellis (1995a) has attempted to encapsulate these dilemmas in a more succinct agenda but he has met considerable opposition. This is not because his proposed values of 'anti-custodialism', 'restorative justice' and 'community safety' are in themselves anathemas to probation officers but because he links them with a demand that the probation service cease to view itself as a social work agency. He has rightly made explicit that the route down which the service has allowed itself to be led has removed it further and further from traditional social work values. But, as Spencer points out (1995), there are costs to this 'paradigm shift' which cannot be assumed to be to the service's ethical advantage. If the probation service adopts this agenda of social and community justice, is there not a danger that the needs of individuals will be lost? And since it seems no more likely in the current political climate that values embedded in notions of social and community justice will be acceptable to policy-makers than the old-fashioned values of casework, is there not also a danger that discarding the familiar for the new could hasten the demise of the probation service altogether?

Nellis, with some justification, rejects this criticism as a wilful misunderstanding and argues that he is trying to refine the values of the probation service, not prescribe an entirely new form of service (1995b). But other criticisms are less easy to dismiss. James (1995) complains that Nellis continues to treat the probation service as though it had a future independent of the rest of the criminal justice system. Recent developments in criminological theory and in managerialism both emphasise the interdependent or corporatist nature of criminal justice agencies. It is naïve (and positivistic) to believe that one agency can provide an independent influence on policy-making. The probation service is part of a system which is increasingly well co-ordinated around a philosophy of 'crime control'. That philosophy, as James points out, is not inherently antipathetic to rehabilitation – provided rehabilitation is applied to the *right* groups of offenders. The problem is not, therefore, that the probation service is fighting a lone battle for the moral high ground – it is more subtle than that. The problem is that fewer and fewer offenders are being deemed 'suitable' for rehabilitative measures.

A thread which runs through Ward and Lacey's collection (1995) is a call for a return to an even older concept of 'justice'. *Probation: Working for Justice* is dedicated to the memory of John Pendleton, former Baptist minister and chief probation officer of Warwickshire. His own essay 'More justice, less law' sets a tone of reconciliation which is followed by all the contributors. First, he argues, we must try to keep as many people as possible out of the criminal justice system because most of the things that need to be done to put wrongs right in society cannot be done through sanctions. Second, if people do have to go to court, then the system should be concerned primarily with 'putting wrongs right' and should see 'custody as the alternative'.

Partnership, corporatism and the decline of influence?

In Chapter 5, brief mention was made of the (pale) Green Paper on *Partnership in Dealing with Offenders in the Community* (Home Office 1990c). Its purpose was to encourage the probation service to see itself as part of a network of both informal and formal agencies within the criminal justice system. Subsequent legislation and the 'Lavender' decision document (Home Office 1992c) reinforced the requirement for the probation service to develop its relationships with the 'independent sector' – a term which controversially included the burgeoning private sector as well as traditional charities and voluntary organisations. Services were required to spend around 5 per cent of their budget on such partnerships. Since that time, probation services have experienced severe cuts in their budgets and have therefore come under greater pressure to 'contract out' aspects of service delivery. Relationships with voluntary organisations have not always been on the basis of equality and tensions have been apparent with those organisations, such as NACRO, the Rainer Foundation, National Children's Home (NCH) and Barnardo's, which are proud of their own traditions and values in their work with offenders. Moreover, in times of financial constraint and pressure to demonstrate 'outcomes', the development of genuine partnerships with organisations working 'in the community' may appear time-consuming and inefficient (Nellis 1995c; Broad 1996).

Of more concern than the micro-economy of partnerships is the shift towards a corporatist agenda which is more concerned with crime containment than crime reduction (Nellis 1995c). Such an approach papers over the cracks of genuine differences and conflicts between those involved in 'crime issues' by making them work together in a constructed collective with supposedly agreed aims and objectives. This artificially created consensus is a key feature of Punishment in the Community discourse (see John Patten's 1988 speech, analysed in Chapter 2) and those who resist incorporation are viewed as behaving in a bizarre and subversive way. It also provides the government with 'a useful alibi and a ready-made set of scapegoats for rising crime in the late 1990s' (Nellis 1995c:291). When partnerships fail through time and money constraints, disagreements about the nature of effectiveness and the methods and objectives of evaluation, and through genuine differences of interest, the government can say that the community has failed to take responsibility for itself.

Resisting transformative power

Tim May (1994) argues that what has happened to the probation service is an example of 'transformative power'. Organisational change has *not* been imposed from outside in any straightforwardly repressive sense. Rather, the transformation has been immanent, in the Foucauldian sense, coursing through the arteries of the organisation, changing things from inside. The tactics have been those of incorporation and persuasion. The organisation has only to be persuaded that it has problems (or 'challenges') and that it is being given permission to pursue the 'opportunities' presented by such 'challenges'. In this pursuit, the organisation finds that it can indeed obtain pleasure from forming new knowledge, creating new ways of doing things, producing measurable outcomes. The process is satisfying and the rewards reinforce the behaviour.

Central to this process and uniquely vulnerable to incorporation is middle management (in this case, senior probation officers) whose task is to establish managerial goals and practices. Seniors are dependent for their survival on incorporation and find it hard to resist the pressure to be accountable – and to hold officers accountable – for the minutiae of their daily work in actuarial, rather than professional, terms.

But front-line workers (probation officers) have much greater opportunity to resist transformation, according to May. First, there still exists (though for how much longer?) a 'binding ethos' that *the* purpose of the job is to *help people*. Appeal to this ethos serves as a justification for dissent, when demands from management lack professional credibility. Second, probation officers work on a daily basis with much more freedom and discretion than do their managers. Much of their time is spent outside the organisation – in courts and prisons and visiting offenders' homes. Many of the people they deal with are not part of the organisation. Their sense of identity or occupational culture (as with police officers and prison officers) is actively anti-managerial and rooted in collective perceptions of the 'reality' of the job.

The problem with this optimistic analysis is that the front-line workers of yesterday are increasingly becoming the managers of tomorrow. By this, I do not mean that they are being promoted. What I mean is that they are increasingly encouraged to view themselves as 'managers' – 'case managers', 'managers of resources' and so on. Increasingly the 'front-line' work is being done by unqualified probation service officers, by volunteers or by 'partner' organisations. As this happens, one more layer of incorporation or transformation is set in place.

Conclusion

This is not to argue that anyone in the probation service wants to lose sight of the 'binding ethos' of helping people. Most chief probation officers want to reconcile the demands of efficiency, effectiveness and economy with a vision of probation officers as 'compulsive understanders' (Fullwood 1996). But 'probation watchers' observe that such reconciliation is no longer – if it ever was – an option. If there is to be any hope for the future of the service, then it must 'rescue the social' and eschew 'rigid standard procedures supported by macho correctionalism and "radical managerialism" ' (Drakeford and Vanstone 1996:19). Instead it must engage with the social worlds which clients inhabit.

SEEING CUSTODY AS THE ALTERNATIVE

Seeing custody as the alternative

Introduction

'Punishment in the Community' has been officially supplanted by the rhetoric of 'Prison Works' (Home Office 1996a). Having moved from a need to demonstrate that 'alternatives to custody' are at least as effective as custody (in the early and mid-1980s) through a more optimistic phase of 'restricting liberty' to an extent 'commensurate with the seriousness of the offence' (in the late 1980s and early 1990s), community penalties (both supervisory and financial) are now actively competing for customers in a market environment in which prison is no longer viewed as the last resort but as one of a range of options. The official (if lame) exhortations to sentencers to avoid imprisonment wherever possible have finally ceased and any remaining inhibitions have been removed. The reoffending rates of those sent to prison, it is claimed, are no worse than for those placed on community penalties (Lloyd, Mair and Hough 1994; Maclean 1995). It is as though the secret fears contained in George Orwell's Room 101 had finally been unlocked and have been found to be less disagreeable than expected.

It is tempting, at the end of a book such as this, to summarise one's arguments with bullet-pointed lists of recommendations or questions for future research. But this is to oversimplify an analysis which is riddled with ambiguities and contradictions. Instead, I will tentatively propose that a fully social analysis of community punishment must involve a debunking of received wisdom. We are not short of research. We have so much research on the effectiveness of rehabilitation programmes that we now have to move to 'meta-analysis' (McGuire 1995b) What we are short of is the political and professional will to take such research seriously unless it is always-already framed in terms of punishment (Maclean 1995).

We might start the process of debunking by asking the following questions:

1 Is the 'Punishment in the Community' experience unique to England and Wales, or can we learn lessons from the experiences of other penal systems?
2 Is the search for an articulated set of 'values', which is distinctively associated (only) with the probation service, any longer a relevant or worthwhile venture?

3 Can the rhetoric of 'partnership', with its managerialist assumptions, yet be subverted to provide a genuinely wider range of services to a genuinely wider range of offenders?

4 Is there any hope that newly-deprofessionalised probation officers might yet resist being reconstructed as 'corrections officers' and opt instead to revive and invest in the modest objectives and effective skills of helping offenders to solve the personal and social problems which make it difficult for them to choose *not* to offend?

At the beginning of this book I said that our conceptual analysis of non-incarcerative sanctions was impoverished by our inability to think of them as anything other than 'alternatives' to prison. I have attempted to show that such sanctions deserve analysis in their own right. But that analysis has not led to the conclusion that they are necessarily 'better', in their present form and content, than prison. On the contrary, to the extent that they blur the boundaries between freedom and captivity, they cease to be genuine 'alternatives' and are merely poor substitutes for the 'real thing'. Life for many offenders at the end of the century is not so good that we can make limitless demands on them in the belief that they will endure anything to avoid prison. And we must stop pretending that the criminal justice system can find the answer to crime. Playing at 'restorative justice' and 'mediation' in a society as grossly unequal as ours is, to mix the metaphors, applying no more than first aid to a gaping wound. Such approaches are *reflections* of a just and confident society but they do not create it. Only when there is a political will to invest in human, social and cultural capital and a willingness for sentencers to see custody as the alternative – the sentence of last resort – will things change.[1]

Two things are clear from comparisons with the experiences of other countries. One is that the role of community punishment as a means of reducing the prison population is a failure. There is no relationship between the use of community punishment and the size of the prison population, *unless*, as with the 1991 Criminal Justice Act, there is a deliberate curbing of the courts' sentencing powers through legislation. Left to their own devices, in the current worldwide obsession with internal law and order, courts find it hard to resist the 'pull' of imprisonment. But it is also true that we do not need to be obsessed with what is happening in America. There are many examples elsewhere of innovative, if modest, schemes which help offenders to see the advantages of choosing not to offend.

The downsizing of the probation service in England and Wales is unlikely to be reversed in the foreseeable future. Amalgamations of services may increase in order to make savings and specific tasks (such as court duties and reports) will be increasingly casualised. Some services have already begun to put a range of services out to tender by independent organisations. Within the current punitive penal climate, it is difficult to argue in favour of such moves. But the probation service does not have a monopoly on caring for offenders and genuine partnership with other organisations that share the service's more traditional ethos must be recognised as one possible way forward.

The probation service will never achieve its ambition to be 'centre-stage' in the criminal justice system and it must stop tilting at the windmills of prison. Punishment in the Community alone will never succeed in reducing the prison population. The mechanisms of discipline 'in the community' are always-already excluded from the discourse of custody – they represent the *Other* of prison talk. Once this is faced up to, it may be possible to unhitch them, once and for all, from their unequal and subordinate relationship with custody, where they are viewed as being effective only in so far as they replicate the pains of imprisonment. They must instead be viewed as constituting a sphere of social control which is quite separate from that of the prison, based on self-government and normalising instruction (Rose 1989). Freed from the constraints of proving effectiveness in relation to prison, community punishments can be tailored to the needs of those towards whom the state has an obligation of advice, assistance or – dare it be said – friendship. Once uncoupled from custody, the accusation that such a vision merely serves to net-widen becomes irrelevant. Net-widening is only to be avoided when the net leads to exclusion from the rights and duties of citizenship. What is wrong with widening the net of skills and knowledge, including social skills and self-knowledge? What is wrong with widening the net of self-esteem, attachment and commitment to the future? What, in short, is wrong with widening the net of inclusion?

Note

1   As I read the proofs for this book on 2 May 1997, there is a change of government. Although it seems unlikely that there will be much immediate change in criminal justice policy, a new political will to invest in human, social and cultural capital may yet secure a more hopeful future for community punishment in general and the probation service in particular.

REFERENCES

Adler, F. (1975) *Sisters in Crime*, New York, McGraw- Hill.

Alderson, J. (1979) *Policing Freedom*, Plymouth, McDonald and Evans.

Allen, H. (1987) *Justice Unbalanced*, Milton Keynes, Open University Press.

Armstrong, S. (1990) *Alternatives to custody? Day centre and community service provision for women*, Occasional Paper 4, University of Keele, Centre for Criminology.

Asquith, S. (ed.)(1993) *Protecting Children: Cleveland to Orkney: More Lessons to Learn?*, Edinburgh, HMSO.

Baird, V. (1996) 'Mandatory thought required', *Criminal Justice*,**14** (2): 4–5.

Baker, S. (1993) *The Rise and Fall of Unit Fines*, unpublished dissertation, Keele University Department of Criminology.

Bale, D. (1987) 'Using a risk of custody scale', *Probation Journal* **34** (4): 127–31.

Barker, M. (1993) *Community Service and Women Offenders*, London, Association of Chief Officers of Probation.

Barker, M. (1995) 'What works with sex offenders?' in G. McIvor (ed.) *Working with Offenders*, Research Highlights in Social Work 26, London, Jessica Kingsley.

Barnett, S., Corder, F. and Jehu, D. (1990) 'Group treatment for women sex offenders against children', *Groupwork*, **3** (2): 191–203.

Beaumont, B. (1995) 'Managerialism and the Probation Service' in B. Williams (ed.) *Probation Values*, Birmingham, Venture Press.

Beck, U. (1992) *Risk Society: Towards a New Modernity*, London, Sage.

Bennett, T. (1994) 'Community policing', *Criminal Justice Matters* **17**: 6–7.

Biestek, F. (1961) *The Casework Relationship*, London, Unwin University Books.

Boswell, G. (1996) *Young and Dangerous: the Background Careers of Section 53 Offenders*, Aldershot, Avebury.

Bottoms, A. (1983) 'Neglected features of contemporary penal systems' in D. Garland and P. Young (eds) *The Power to Punish*, London, Heinemann.

Bottoms, A. (1995) 'The philosophy and politics of punishment and sentencing' in C. Clarkson and R. Morgan (eds) *The Politics of Sentencing Reform*, Oxford, Clarendon Press.

Bottoms, A. and McWilliams, W. (1979) 'A non-treatment paradigm for probation practice', *British Journal Social Work*, **9** (2): 159–202.

Bottoms, A. and Stelman, A. (1988) *Social Inquiry Reports*, Aldershot, Wildwood House.

Box, S. (1987) *Recession, Crime and Punishment*, London, Macmillan.

Braithwaite, J. (1989) *Crime, Shame and Reintegration*, Cambridge, Cambridge University Press.

Brinkworth,L. (1994) 'Sugar and spice but not at all nice', *The Sunday Times*, 27 November.

Broad, B. (1991) *Punishment under Pressure*, London, Jessica Kingsley.

Broad, B. (1996) 'New partnerships in work with offenders and crime prevention work', in T. May and A.A. Vass (eds) *Working with Offenders: Issues, Contexts and Outcomes*, London, Sage.

Brown, S. (1990) *Magistrates at Work*, Milton Keynes, Open University Press.

Buchanan, J., Collett, S. and McMullan, P. (1991) 'Challenging practice or challenging women? Female offenders and illicit drug use', *Probation Journal*, **38** (2): 56–62.

Burgess, A. (1962) *A Clockwork Orange*, Harmondsworth, Penguin Books.

Byrne, J.M., Lurigio, A.J. and Petersilia, J. (1992) *Smart Sentencing: the Emergence of Intermediate Sanctions*, London, Sage.

Cambridge Institute of Criminology (1990) *National Survey of Intermediate Treatment*, Cambridge, Institute of Criminology.

Campbell, B. (1988) *Unofficial Secrets*, London, Virago Press.

Campbell, B. (1993) *Goliath: Britain's Dangerous Places*, London, Methuen.

Carlen, P. (1976) *Magistrates' Justice*, London, Routledge Kegan Paul.

Carlen,P. (1988) *Women, Crime and Poverty*, Milton Keynes, Open University Press.

Carlen, P. (1989) 'Crime, inequality and sentencing' in P. Carlen, P. and D. Cook, (eds) *Paying for Crime*, Milton Keynes, Open University Press.

Carlen, P. (1990) *Alternatives to women's imprisonment*, Buckingham, Open University Press.

Carlen, P. and Powell, M. (1979) 'Professionals in the magistrates courts' in H.Parker (ed.) *Social Work and the Courts*, London, Edward Arnold.

Cavadino, M. and Dignan, J. (1992) *The Penal System: An Introduction*, London, Sage.

Cavadino, P. (ed.) (1996) *Children Who Kill*, Winchester, Waterside Press.

Chapman, T. (1995) 'Creating a culture of change: a case study of a car crime project in Belfast', in J. McGuire (ed.) *What Works: Reducing Reoffending*, Chichester, John Wiley.

Charles, N., Whittaker, C. and Ball, C. (1997) *Sentencing without a Pre-Sentence Report*, Home Office Research Findings 47, London, HMSO.

Chiqwada, R. (1989) 'The criminalisation and imprisonment of black women', *Probation Journal*, **36** (3): 100–105.

Cohen, S. (1979) 'The punitive city: notes on the dispersal of social control', *Contemporary Crises*, **3**: 339–63.

Cohen, S. (1983) 'Social control talk: telling stories about correctional change' in D. Garland and P. Young (eds) *The Power to Punish*, London, Heinemann.

Cohen, S. (1985) *Visions of Social Control*, Cambridge, Polity Press.

Coulshed, V. (1988) *Social Work Practice: an Introduction*, London, Macmillan.

Cowburn, M. and Modi, P. (1995) 'Justice in an unjust context: implications for working with adult male sex offenders' in D. Ward and M. Lacey (eds) *Probation: Working for Justice*, London, Whiting & Birch.

Curnock, K. and Hardiker, P. (1979) *Towards Practice Theory*, London, Routledge Kegan Paul.

Davies, M., Croall, H. and Tyrer, J. (1995) *Criminal Justice*, Harlow, Longman.

Denney, D. (1992) *Racism and Anti-Racism in the Probation Service*, London, Routledge.

Department of Health/Home Office (1992) *Report of Health and Social Services for Mentally Disordered Offenders* (Reed Report) Cmnd. 2088, London, HMSO.

Dominelli, L. (1984) 'Differential justice: domestic labour, community service and female offenders', *Probation Journal*, **31** (3): 100–103.

Donzelot, J. (1980) *The Policing of Families*, London, Hutchinson.

Drakeford, M. (1993) 'The probation service, breach and the Criminal Justice Act 1991', *The Howard Journal of Criminal Justice*, **32** (4): 291–303.

Drakeford, M. and Vanstone, M. (1996) 'Rescuing the social', *Probation Journal*, **43** (1): 16–19.

Duguid, G. (1982) *Community Service in Scotland: The First Two Years*, Edinburgh, Scottish Office Central Research Unit.

Dunkley, C. (1992) *Groupwork with Women in Probation Day Centres*, University of Manchester, Department of Social Policy and Social Work.

Eaton, M. (1985) 'Documenting the defendant: placing women in social inquiry reports', in J. Brophy and C. Smart (eds) *Women in Law*, London, Routledge Kegan Paul.

Eaton, M. (1986) *Justice for Women?*, Milton Keynes, Open University Press.

Eaton, M. (1993) *Women after Prison*, Milton Keynes, Open University Press.

Evans, K., Fraser, P. and Walklate, S. (1996) 'Whom can you trust? The politics of ''grassing'' on an inner city housing estate', *Sociological Review*, **44** (3) 361–380.

Fatic, A. (1995) *Punishment and Restorative Crime-Handling: a Social Theory of Trust*, Aldershot, Avebury.

Faulkner, D. (1993) 'All flaws and disorder', *Guardian*, 11 November.

Faulkner, D. (1996) *Darkness and Light: Justice, Crime and Management for Today*, London, The Howard League for Penal Reform.

Folkard, M.S., Smith, D.E. and Smith, D.D. (1976) *IMPACT: Intensive Matched Probation and After-Care Treatment*, Home Office Research Study 36, London, HMSO.

Forbes, J. (1992) 'Female sexual abusers: the contemporary search for equivalence', *Practice*, **6** (2): 102–11.

Forrester, D., Chatterton, M. and Pease, K. (1988) *The Kirkholt Burglary Prevention Project, Rochdale*, Crime Prevention Unit Paper 13, London, Home Office.

Foucault, M. (1977) *Discipline and Punish*, London, Allen Lane.

Frazer, E. and Lacey, N. (1993) *The Politics of Community: A Feminist Critique of the Liberal-Communitarian Debate*, London, Harvester Wheatsheaf.

Fullwood, C. (1996) 'The future of the probation service: the case for the compulsive understander', *Probation Journal*, **43** (3) 118–26.

Gallo, E. (1995) 'The penal system in France: from correctionalism to managerialism' in V. Ruggiero, M. Ryan and J. Sim (eds) *Western European Penal Systems: a Critical Anatomy*, London, Sage.

Gardiner, S. (1995) 'Criminal Justice Act 1991 – management of the underclass and the potentiality of community', in L. Noaks, M. Levi and M. Maguire (eds) *Contemporary Issues in Criminology*, Cardiff, University of Wales Press.

Garland, D. (1985) *Punishment and Welfare: A History of Penal Strategies*, Aldershot, Gower.

Garland, D. (1990) *Punishment and Modern Society*, Oxford, Oxford University Press.

Garland, D. (1995) 'Panopticon days', *Criminal Justice Matters*, No. 20, Summer, 3–4.

Gelsthorpe, L. and Tutt, N. (1986) 'The Attendance Centre Order', *Criminal Law Review*, 146–53.

Genders, E. and Player, E. (1995) *Grendon: a Study of a Therapeutic Prison*, Oxford, Clarendon Press.

Gibson, B., Cavadino, P., Rutherford, A., Ashworth, A. and Harding, J. (1994) *Criminal Justice in Transition*, Winchester, Waterside Press.

Gillis, J.G. (1974) *Youth and History*, New York, Academic Press.

Gilyeat, D. (1993) *A Companion Guide to Offence Seriousness*, Ilkley, Owen Wells Publisher.

Gocke, B. (1995) 'Working with people who have committed sexual offences' in B. Williams (ed.) *Probation Values*, Birmingham, Venture Press.

Goffman, E. (1961) *Asylums*, Harmondsworth, Penguin Books.

Golding, W. (1960) *Lord of the Flies*, Harmondsworth, Penguin Books.

Gordon, C. (1979) 'Other inquisitions', *Ideology and Consciousness*, **6**: 23–46.

Groombridge, N. (1995) 'Candid cameras', *Criminal Justice Matters* No. 20, Summer, 9.

Hagan, J. (1994) *Crime and Disrepute*, Thousand Oaks, Pine Forge.

Hagell, A. and Newburn, T. (1994) *Persistent Young Offenders*, London, Policy Studies Institute.

Hamai, F. and Ville, R. (1995) 'Volunteer probation personnel', in F. Hamai, R. Ville, M. Hough, R. Harris and U. Zveckic (eds) *Probation Around the World*, London, Routledge.

Hamai, F., Ville, R., Harris, R., Hough, M. and Zvekic, U. (eds) (1995) *Probation Around the World*, London, Routledge.

Hardiker, P. and Willis, A. (1989) 'Cloning probation officers: consumer research and implications for training', *The Howard Journal of Criminal Justice*, **28** (4): 323–9.

Harris, R. (1980) 'A changing service: the case for separating care and control in probation practice', *British Journal of Social Work*, **10** (2): 163–84.

Harris, R. (1992) *Crime, Criminal Justice and the Probation Service*, London, Routledge.

Harris, R. (1995) 'Studying probation: a comparative approach' and 'Reflections on comparative probation', in F. Hamai, R. Ville, M. Hough, R. Harris and U. Zveckic (eds) *Probation Around the World*, London, Routledge.

Haxby, D. (1978) *Probation: a Changing Service*, London, Constable.

Hay, C. (1995) 'Mobilization through interpellation: James Bulger, juvenile crime and the construction of a moral panic', *Social and Legal Studies*, **4** (2): 197–223.

Hayman, S. (1996) *Community Prisons for Women*, London, Prison Reform Trust.

Hebenton, B. and Thomas, T. (1996) 'Tracking sex offenders', *The Howard Journal of Criminal Justice*, **35** (2) 97–112.

Hedderman, C. and Hough, M. (1994) *Does the Criminal Justice System Treat Men and Women Differently?*, Home Office Research Findings 10, London, HMSO.

Hedderman, C. and Sugg, D. (1996) *Does Treating Sex Offenders Reduce Reoffending?*, Home Office Research Findings 45, London, HMSO.

Heidensohn, F. (1985) *Women and Crime*, Basingstoke, Macmillan.

HM Inspectorate of Probation (1991) *The Work of the Probation Service with Sex Offenders: Report of a Thematic Inspection*, London, Home Office.

HM Inspectorate of Probation (1993) *Approved Probation and Bail Hostels: Report of a Thematic Inspection*, London, Home Office.

Hine, J. (1993) 'Access for women: flexible and friendly?' in D. Whitfield and D. Scott (eds) *Paying Back: Twenty Years of Community Service*, Winchester, Waterside Press.

Hine, J. and Thomas, N. (1995) 'Evaluating Work with Offenders: Community Service Orders' in G. McIvor (ed.) *Working with Offenders*, Research Highlights in Social Work 26, London, Jessica Kingsley.

Home Office (1988) *Punishment, Custody and the Community*, Cmnd. 424, London, HMSO.

Home Office (1990a) *Crime, Justice and Protecting the Public*, Cmnd. 965, London, HMSO.

Home Office (1990b) *Supervision and Punishment in the Community*, Cmnd. 966, London, HMSO.

Home Office (1990c) *Partnership in Dealing with Offenders in the Community*, London, HMSO.

Home Office (1991) *Organising Supervision and Punishment in the Community: a Decision Document*, London, HMSO.

Home Office (1992a) *Section 95: Gender and the Criminal Justice System*, London, Home Office.

Home Office (1992b) *National Standards for the Supervision of Offenders in the Community*, London, Home Office.

Home Office (1992c) *Partnership in Dealing with Offenders in the Community: a Decision Document*, London, HMSO.

Home Office (1993) *Monitoring of the Criminal Justice Act 1991*, Statistical Bulletin 25/93, London, Home Office.

Home Office (1994a) *Criminal Statistics England and Wales 1993*, London, HMSO.

Home Office (1994b) *Probation Statistics England and Wales 1993*, London, Home Office.

Home Office (1995a) *Cautions, Court Proceedings and Sentencing England and Wales 1994*, Home Office Statistical Bulletin 18/95, London, Home Office.

Home Office (1995b) *Statistics of Mentally Disordered Offenders England and Wales 1994*, Home Office Statistical Bulletin 20/95, London, Home Office.

Home Office (1995c) *Strengthening Punishment in the Community*, Cmnd. 2780, London, HMSO.

Home Office (1995d) *Digest 3: Information on the Criminal Justice System in England and Wales*, London, Home Office.

Home Office (1995e) *National Standards for the Supervision of Offenders in the Community*, London, Home Office.

Home Office (1996a) *Protecting the Public*, Cmnd. 3190, London, HMSO.

Home Office (1996b) *Probation Statistics England and Wales 1994,* London, Home Office.

Home Office (1996c) *Summary Probation Statistics England and Wales 1995*, Home Office Statistical Bulletin 10/96, London, Home Office.

Hood, R. (1992) *Race and Sentencing*, Oxford, Clarendon Press.

Hope, T. (1995) 'Building a safer society: Strategic approaches to crime prevention', in M. Tonry and D.P. Farrington (eds) *Crime and Justice: Volume 19*, Chicago, University of Chicago Press.

Howe, A. (1994) *Punish and Critique*, London, Routledge.

Howe, A., Johnson, B., Purser, B. and Read, G. (1982) 'Establishing day centres', *Probation Journal*, **29** (2): 60–61.

Hudson, A. (1989) 'Troublesome girls,' in M. Cain (ed.) *Growing Up Good*, London, Sage.

Hudson, B. (1987) *Justice through Punishment*, Basingstoke, Macmillan.

Humphrey, C. (1991) 'Calling on the experts', *The Howard Journal of Criminal Justice*, **30** (1): 1–18.

Humphrey, C. and Pease, K. (1992) 'Effectiveness measurement in the Probation Service: a view from the troops', *The Howard Journal of Criminal Justice*, **31** (1): 31–52.

Hutton, W. (1995) *The State We're In*, London, Jonathan Cape.

Ireland, P. (1995) 'Reflections on a rampage through the barriers of shame: law, community and the new conservatism', *Journal of Law and Society*, **22** (2): 189–211.

Jackson, H. and Smith, L. (1987) *Female Offenders: an Analysis of Social Inquiry Reports*, Home Office Research Bulletin 23, London, HMSO.

James, A.C. and Neil, P. (1996) 'Juvenile sexual offending: one-year period prevalence study within Oxfordshire', *Child Abuse and Neglect*, **20** (6): 477–85.

James, A.L. (1995) 'Probation values for the 1990s – and beyond?', *The Howard Journal of Criminal Justice*, **34** (4): 326–43.

James, J. and Thornton, W. (1980) 'Women's liberation and the female delinquent', *Journal of Research in Crime and Delinquency*, 230–44.

Jones, C. (1983) *State Social Work and the Working Class*, London, Macmillan.

Jones, M., Mordecai, M., Rutter, F. and Thomas, L. (1991) 'The Miskin Model of groupwork with women offenders', *Groupwork*, **4** (3): 215–30.

Katz, J. (1988) *Seductions of Crime: Moral and Sensual Attractions in Doing Evil*, New York, Basic Books.

Kemshall, H. (1995) 'Risk in probation practice', *Probation Journal* **42** (2): 67–72.

Kemshall, H. (1996) 'Risk assessment: fuzzy thinking or decisions in action?', *Probation Journal*, **43** (1) 2–7.

King, R. (1995) 'Woodcock and after', *Prison Service Journal*, **102**: 63–7.

Kirwin, K. (1985) 'Probation and supervision', in H. Walker and B. Beaumont (eds) *Working with Offenders*, London, Macmillan.

Knott, C. (1995) 'The STOP programme: reasoning and habilitation in a British setting', in J. McGuire, (ed.) *What Works: Reducing Reoffending*, Chichester, John Wiley.

Kosh, M. and Williams, B. (1995) *The Probation Service and Victims of Crime: a Pilot Study*, Keele, Keele University Press.

Lacey, M. (1984) 'Intermediate treatment: a theory for practice', *Probation Journal*, **31** (3): 104–107.

Lawrence,D. (1995) 'Race, culture and the probation service', in G. McIvor (ed.) *Working with Offenders*, Research Highlights in Social Work 26, London, Jessica Kingsley.

Lawson, C. (1978) *The Probation Officer as Prosecutor*, Cambridge, Institute of Criminology, University of Cambridge.

Lea, J. and Young, J. (1984) *What Is to be Done about Law and Order?*, Harmondsworth, Penguin Books.

Leander, K. (1995) 'The normalization of Swedish prisons', in V. Ruggiero, M. Ryan and J. Sim (eds) *Western European Penal Systems: a Critical Anatomy*, London, Sage.

Lees, S. (1993) *Sugar and Spice*, Harmondsworth, Penguin Books.

Lees, S. (1997) *Ruling Passions: Sexual Violence, Reputation and the Law*, Milton Keynes, Open University Press.

Le Mesurier, L. (1935) *A Handbook of Probation*, London, NAPO.

Lishman, J. (1991) *Handbook of Theory for Practice Teachers in Social Work*, London, Jessica Kingsley.

Lloyd, S., Farrell, G. and Pease, K. (1994) *Preventing Repeated Domestic Violence: a Demonstration Project on Merseyside*, Police Research Group Crime Prevention Unit Series, Paper 49, London, Home Office.

Lloyd, C., Mair, G. and Hough, M. (1994) *Explaining Reconviction Rates: a Critical Analysis*, Home Office Research Study 136, London, HMSO.

Loader, I. (1996) *Youth, Policing and Democracy*, London, Macmillan.

McCorry, J. and Morrissey, M. (1989) 'Community, crime and punishment in West Belfast', *The Howard Journal of Criminal Justice*, **28** (4): 282–290.

McConville, B. (1983) *Women under the Influence*, London, Virago.

McGuire, J. (ed.) (1995a) *What Works: Reducing Reoffending*, Chichester, John Wiley.

McGuire, J. (1995b) 'The failure of punishment', *Science and Public Affairs*, Winter, 37–40.

McGuire, J. and Priestley, P. (1985) *Offending Behaviour: Skills and Strategems for Going Straight*, London, Batsford.

McIvor, G. (1992) *Sentenced to Serve*, Aldershot, Avebury.

McLoone, P., Oulds, G. and Morris, J. (1987) 'Alcohol education groups: compulsion v. voluntarism', *Probation Journal*, **34** (1): 25.

McNeill, S. (1987) 'Flashing: its effects on women', in J. Hanmer and M. Maynard (eds) *Women, Violence and Social Control*, Basingstoke, Macmillan.

McWilliams, W. (1990) 'Probation practice and the management ideal', *Probation Journal*, **37** (2): 60–7.

McWilliams, W. (1992) 'The rise and development of management thought in the English probation system', in R.Statham and P.Whitehead (eds) *Managing the Probation Service: Issues for the 1990s*, Harlow, Longman.

Maclean, D. (1995) 'Deterrence works', *Science and Public Affairs*, Winter, 41.

Magistrates' Association (1993) 'Sentencing guidelines', in B. Gibson *et al.* (1994) *Criminal Justice in Transition*, Winchester, Waterside Press.

Mair, G. (1988) *Probation Day Centres*, Home Office Research Study 100, London, HMSO.

Mair, G. (1995) 'Specialist activities in probation: confusion worse confounded?' in L. Noaks, M. Levi and M. Maguire (eds) *Issues in Contemporary Criminology*, Cardiff, University of Wales Press.

Mair, G. and Brockington, N. (1988) 'Female offenders and the probation service', *The Howard Journal of Criminal Justice*, **27** (2): 117–26.

Mair, G., Lloyd, C., Nee, C. and Sibbitt, R. (1994) *Intensive Probation in England and Wales: an Evaluation*, Home Office Research Study 133, London, HMSO.

Martin, C. and Godfrey, D. (1994) 'Prisoners' views of Boards of Visitors', *British Journal of Criminology*, **34** (3): 358–65.

Martinson, R. (1974) 'What works? Questions and answers about prison reform', *The Public Interest*, **35** 22–54.

Masters, R.E. (1994) *Counseling Criminal Justice Offenders*, Thousand Oaks, Sage.

Mathiesen, T. (1983) 'The future of control systems', in D. Garland, and P. Young, (eds) *The Power to Punish*, London, Heinemann.

Matthews, R. (1990) 'New directions in the privatization debate?' *Probation Journal*, **37** (2): 50–59.

May, T. (1991) *Probation: Politics, Policy and Practice*, Buckingham, Open University Press.

May, T. (1994) 'Transformative power: a study in a human service organization', *The Sociological Review*, **42** (2) 618–38.

Mawby, R. and Walklate, S. (1994) *Critical Victimology*, London, Sage.

Messner, C. and Ruggiero, V. (1995) 'Germany: the penal system between past and future' in V. Ruggiero, M. Ryan and J. Sim (eds) *Western European Penal Systems: a Critical Anatomy*, London, Sage.

Millard, D. (1982) 'Keeping the probation service whole: the case for discretion', *British Journal of Social Work*, **12** :291–301.

Mistry, T. (1989) 'Establishing a feminist model of groupwork in the probation service', *Groupwork*, **2**: 145–58.

Moloney, N. (1995) *Combination Orders: their History, Use and Impact*, Social Work Monograph 137, Norwich, University of East Anglia.

Morris, A. (1987) *Women, Crime and Criminal Justice*, Oxford, Basil Blackwell.

Morris, A., Giller, H., Szwed, E. and Geach, H. (1980) *Justice for Children*, London, Macmillan.

Morton, J. (1994) *A Guide to the Criminal Justice and Public Order Act 1994*, London, Butterworths.

Moxon, D. (1995) 'England abandons unit fines', in M. Tonry, and K. Hamilton (eds) *Intermediate Sanctions in Overcrowded Times*, Boston, Northeastern University Press.

Murray, C. (1990) 'Underclass' in *The Emerging British Underclass*, London, Institute of Economic Affairs.

NACRO (1989) *The Real Alternative: Strategies to Promote Community-Based Penalties*, London, NACRO.

NACRO (1994) *Community Prisons*, London, NACRO.

NACRO (1996) *Criminal Justice Digest*, No 90, October.

NAPO (1992) *NAPO News*, March.

NAPO (1993) *NAPO News*, February.

NAPO (1994) *NAPO News*, May.

NAPO (1996) *NAPO News*, February.

NAPO (1997) *NAPO News*, January.

Nellis, M. (1989) 'Keeping tags on the underclass', *Social Work Today*, **20** (37): 18–19.

Nellis, M. (1991) 'The last days of juvenile justice', in P. Carter, T. Jeffs and M. Smith (eds) *Social Work and Social Welfare Yearbook 3*, Buckingham, Open University Press.

Nellis, M. (1995a) 'Probation values for the 1990s', *The Howard Journal of Criminal Justice*, **34**, (1): 19–44.

Nellis, M. (1995b) 'The "third way" for probation: a reply to Spencer and James', *The Howard Journal of Criminal Justice*, **34** (3): 350–3.

Nellis, M. (1995c) 'Partnership, punishment and justice', in D. Ward and M. Lacey, (eds) *Probation: Working for Justice*, London, Whiting & Birch.

Newburn, T. (1995) *Crime and Criminal Justice Policy*, London, Longman.

Oldfield, M. (1993) 'Assessing the impact of community service: lost opportunities and the politics of punishment', in D. Whitfield and D. Scott (eds) *Paying Back: Twenty Years of Community Service*, Winchester, Waterside Press.

O'Mahony, D. and Haines, K. (1996) *An Evaluation of the Introduction and Operation of the Youth Court*, Home Office Research Study 152, London, HMSO.

Orwell. G. (1949) *Nineteen Eighty Four*, Harmondsworth, Penguin Books.

Owen, L. and Morris-Jones, R. (1988) 'They don't come voluntarily, do they?', *Probation Journal*, **35** (1) 30–31.

Parker, H. (1988) 'Greenpapering over the cracks', Paper presented to Management Study Day, Greater Manchester Probation Service, 4 October.

Parker, H., Sumner, M. and Jarvis, G. (1989) *Unmasking the Magistrates*, Milton Keynes, Open University Press.

Patten, J. (1988) 'Punishment, the Probation Service and the Community', Speech to Association of Chief Officers of Probation, Home Office, 15 September.

Pearson, G. (1983) *Hooligan: A History of Respectable Fears*, London, Macmillan.

Pearson, G. (1994) 'Youth, crime and society' in M. Maguire, R. Morgan and R. Reiner (eds) *The Oxford Handbook of Criminology*, Oxford, Clarendon Press.

Pease, K. (1983) 'Penal innovations', in J. Lishman (ed.) *Social Work with Adult Offenders*, Research Highlights No 5, Aberdeen, University of Aberdeen.

Pease, K. (1992) 'Preface', in R. Statham and P. Whitehead (eds) *Managing the Probation Service: Issues for the 1990s*, Harlow, Longman.

Pease, K. and Bottomley, K. (1986) *Crime and Punishment: Interpreting the Data*, Milton Keynes, Open University Press.

Pease, K. and McWilliams, W. (1977) 'Assessing community service schemes: pitfalls for the unwary', *Probation Journal*, **24** (4): 137–9.

Pease, K. *et al.* (1975) *Community Service Orders*, Home Office Research Study 29, London, HMSO.

Peckham, A. (1985) *A Woman in Custody*, London, Fontana.

Penal Affairs Consortium (1994) *The Path to Community Prisons*, London, Penal Affairs Consortium.

Penal Affairs Consortium (1995) *Doli Incapax*, London, Penal Affairs Consortium.

Perry, F. (1979) *Reports for Criminal Courts*, Ilkley, Owen Wells.

Phillpotts, G. and Lancucki, L.B. (1979) *Previous Convictions, Sentence and Reconvictions*, Home Office Research Study 53, London, HMSO.

Pitts, J. (1986) 'Black young people and juvenile crime: some unanswered questions', in R. Matthews and J. Young (eds) *Confronting Crime*, London, Sage.

Pitts, J. (1990) *Working with Young Offenders*, London, Macmillan.

Pitts, J. (1992a) 'Juvenile justice policy in England and Wales', in J.C. Coleman and C. Warren-Adamson (eds) *Youth Policy in the 1990s*, London, Routledge.

Pitts, J. (1992b) 'The end of an era', *The Howard Journal of Criminal Justice*, **31** (2): 133–49.

Pitts, J. (1993) 'Theorotyping: anti-racism, criminology and black young people', in D. Cook and B. Hudson (eds) *Racism and Criminology*, London, Sage.

Platt, A. (1969) *The Child Savers*, Chicago, University of Chicago Press.

Prison Reform Trust (1990a) *Comments on the White Paper 'Crime, Justice and Protecting the Public'*, London, Prison Reform Trust.

Prison Reform Trust (1990b) *Sex Offenders in Prison*, London, Prison Reform Trust

Raynor, P. (1978) 'Compulsory persuasion: a problem for correctional social work', *British Journal of Social Work*, **8** (4): 411–24.

Raynor, P. (1985) *Social Work, Justice and Control*, Oxford, Basil Blackwell.

Raynor, P. (1992) *Straight Thinking on Probation: One Year On*, Bridgend, Mid-Glamorgan Probation Service.

Raynor, P. and Vanstone, M. (1994) *Straight Thinking on Probation: Third Interim Evaluation Report*, Bridgend, Mid-Glamorgan Probation Service.

Raynor, P., Smith, D. and Vanstone, M. (1994) *Effective Probation Practice*, London, Macmillan.

Reiner, R. (1989) 'Race and criminal justice', *New Community*, **16** (1): 5–21.

Reiner, R. (1994) 'Policing and the police', in M. Maguire, R. Morgan and R. Reiner (eds) *The Oxford Handbook of Criminology*, Oxford, Clarendon Press.

Richardson, G. (1990) 'Juvenile sexual perpetrators: a model approach and the role of the probation service', *Probation Journal*, **37** (4): 150–58.

Roberts, J. (1994) 'The relationship between the community and the prison' in E. Player and M. Jenkins (eds) *Prisons after Woolf*, London, Routledge.

Rose, N. (1989) *Governing the Soul*, London, Routledge.

Ross, R. and Fabiano, E. (1989) *Reasoning and Rehabilitation: a Handbook for Teaching Cognitive Skills*, Ottawa, The Cognitive Centre.

Rutherford, A. (1986) *Growing out of Crime*, Harmondsworth, Penguin Books.

Sampson, A. (1994) *Acts of Abuse*, London, Routledge.

Sanders, A. and Senior, P. (eds) (1994) *Jarvis' Probation Service Manual*, 5th edn, Sheffield, PAVIC Publications.

Scarborough, J., Geraghty, J. and Loffhagen, J. (1987) 'Day centres and voluntarism', *Probation Journal*, **34** (2): 47–50.

Scull, A. (1977/1984) *Decarceration: Community Treatment and the Deviant*, Cambridge, Polity Press.

Senior, P. (1985) 'Groupwork with offenders' in H. Walker and B. Beaumont (eds) *Working with offenders*, Basingstoke, Macmillan.

Shapland, J. and Vagg, J. (1988) *Policing by the Public*, London, Routledge.

Shaw, K. (1987) 'Skills, control and the mass professions', *The Sociological Review*, **35** (4): 775–93.

Sheath, M. (1990) 'Confrontative work with sex offenders: legitimised nonce-bashing?', *Probation Journal*, **37** (4): 159–62.

Shepherd, G. (1991) 'Management: short of ideals?', *Probation Journal*, **37** (4) 176–81.

Sim, J. (1994) 'Reforming the penal wasteland? A critical review of the Woolf Report' in E. Player and M. Jenkins (eds) *Prisons after Woolf*, London, Routledge.

Sim, J., Ruggiero, V. and Ryan, M. (1995) 'Punishment in Europe: perceptions and commonalities', in V. Ruggiero, M. Ryan and J. Sim (eds) *Western European Penal Systems: a Critical Anatomy*, London, Sage.

Smart, B. (1983) 'On discipline and social regulation: a review of Foucault's genealogical analysis', in D. Garland and P. Young (eds) *The Power to Punish*, London, Heinemann.

Smith, D. (1987) 'The police and the idea of community', in P. Willmott (ed.) *Policing and the Community*, London, Policy Studies Institute.

Smith, D. (1995) *Criminology for Social Work*, London, Macmillan.

Smith, L. (1989) *Concerns about Rape*, Home Office Research Study No. 106, London, HMSO.

Spencer, J. (1995) 'A response to Mike Nellis: probation values for the 1990s', *The Howard Journal of Criminal Justice*, **34** (4): 344–9.

Stacey, T. (1989) 'Why tagging should be used to reduce incarceration', *Social Work Today*, **20** (32): 18–19.

Stephen, J. (1993) *The Misrepresentation of Women Offenders*, Social Work Monograph 118, Norwich, University of East Anglia.

Taylor, I., Walton, P. and Young, J. (1972) *The New Criminology*, London, Routledge.

Thorpe, J. (1979) *Social Enquiry Reports: a Survey*, Home Office Research Study 48, London, HMSO.

Tonry, M. and Hamilton, K. (eds) (1995) *Intermediate Sanctions in Overcrowded Times*, Boston, Northeastern University Press.

Trotter, C. (1995) 'The supervision of offenders – what works?' in L. Noaks, M. Levi and M. Maguire (eds) *Issues in Contemporary Criminology*, Cardiff, University of Wales Press.

Tutt, N. and Giller, H. (1984) *Social Inquiry Reports*, Lancaster, Social Information Systems (tape recording).

van Swaaningen, R. and de Jonge, G. (1995) 'The Dutch prison system and penal policy in the 1990s: from humanitarian paternalism to penal business management' in V. Ruggiero, M. Ryan and J. Sim (eds) *Western European Penal Systems: a Critical Anatomy*, London, Sage.

Vass, A.A. (1990) *Alternatives to Prison*, London, Sage.

von Hirsch, A. and Ashworth, A. (eds) (1992) *Principled Sentencing*, Edinburgh, Edinburgh University Press.

Waite, I. (1994) 'Too little, too bad', *Probation Journal*, **41** (2): 92–4.

Walker, N. (1991) *Why punish?*, Oxford, Oxford University Press.

Walker, H. and Beaumont, B. (1981) *Probation Work: Critical Theory and Socialist Practice,* Oxford, Blackwell.

Walker, H. and Beaumont, B. (1985) *Working with Offenders*, London, Macmillan.

Walklate,S. (1996) 'Community and crime prevention' in E. McLaughlin and J. Muncie (eds) *Controlling Crime*, London, Sage.

Walmsley, R., Howard, L. and White, S. (1992) *The National Prison Survey 1991,* Home Office Research Study 128, London, HMSO.

Ward, D. and Lacey, M. (eds) (1995) *Probation:Working for Justice*, London, Whiting & Birch.

Ward, D. and Spencer, J. (1994) 'The future of probation qualifying training', *Probation Journal*, **41** (2): 95–8.

Weatheritt, M. (1987) 'Community policing now' in P. Willmott (ed.) *Policing and the Community*, London, Policy Studies Institute.

Webb, T. (1996) 'Reconviction prediction for probationers', *Probation Journal*, **43** (1): 8–12.

Welldon, E. (1996) 'Female sex offenders', *Prison Service Journal* **107**: 39–47.

White, I. (1984) 'Residential work: the Cinderella of the probation service?', *Probation Journal*, **31** (2): 59–60.

Whitfield, D. (1993) 'Extending the boundaries', in D. Whitfield and D. Scott (eds) *Paying Back: Twenty Years of Community Service*, Winchester, Waterside Press.

Whitfield, D. (1995) 'Crime, surveillance and tagging: the thin end of the white elephant', *Criminal Justice Matters*, No. 20, Summer, 19.

Whitfield, D. and Scott, D. (eds) (1993) *Paying Back: Twenty Years of Community Service*, Winchester, Waterside Press.

Williams, B. (1994) 'Probation training in the UK: from charity organisation to jobs for the boys', *Social Work Education*, **13** (3): 99–108.

Williams, B. (ed.) (1995) *Probation Values*, Birmingham, Venture Press.

Williams, B. (1996a) *Freedom on Probation*, London, The Association of University Teachers.

Williams, B. (1996b) *Counselling in Criminal Justice*, Buckingham, Open University Press.

Willmott, P. (1987) 'Introduction', in P. Willmott (ed.) *Policing and the Community*, London, Policy Studies Institute.

Wincup, E. (1996) 'Mixed hostels: staff and resident perspectives', *Probation Journal*, **43** (3): 147–51.

Windlesham, Lord (1993) *Responses to Crime*, Vol. 2, Oxford, Oxford University Press.

Woolf, H. and Tumim, S. (1991) *Report into the Prison Disturbances* April 1990, Cmnd. 1456, London, HMSO.

Worrall, A. (1981) 'Out of place: female offenders in court', *Probation Journal*, **28** (3): 90–93.

Worrall, A. (1990/1995) *Offending Women: Female Lawbreakers and the Criminal Justice System*, London, Routledge.

Worrall, A. (1994a) *Have you Got a Minute? The Changing Role of Prison Boards of Visitors*, London, Prison Reform Trust.

Worrall, A. (1994b) 'Magistrates and Prison Boards of Visitors: extended family or only distant relatives?', *The Magistrate*, Vol. 50, No. 8, 157 and 165.

Worrall, A. (1996a) 'Gender, criminal justice and probation', in G. McIvor (ed.) *Working with Offenders*, Research Highlights in Social Work 26, London, Jessica Kingsley.

Worrall, A. (1996b) 'Of rats and real men? prison as community', *Prison Service Journal*, **108**: 58–61.

Young, P.(1989) 'Punishment, money and a sense of justice', in P. Carlen and D. Cook (eds) *Paying for Crime*, Milton Keynes, Open University Press.

INDEX